Image and Response in Early Europe

DUCKWORTH DEBATES IN ARCHAEOLOGY
Series editor: Richard Hodges

Image and Response
in
Early Europe

Peter S. Wells

Duckworth

First published in 2008 by
Gerald Duckworth & Co. Ltd.
90-93 Cowcross Street, London EC1M 6BF
Tel: 020 7490 7300
Fax: 020 7490 0080
inquiries@duckworth-publishers.co.uk
www.ducknet.co.uk

A catalogue record for this book is available
from the British Library

ISBN 978 0 7156 3682 4

Typeset by Ray Davies

Contents

List of illustrations

Sources and credits

3.1. From Dalton 1923, p. 30 fig. 22, used by permission of the Trustees of the British Museum. **3.2.** Top: from Engelhardt 1869, pl. 8, 45-7. Middle: from Engelhardt 1863, pl. 10, 35-7. Bottom: from Engelhardt 1869, pl. 12, 21. **4.1.** From Déchelette 1913, p. 857 fig. 356, 3. **4.3.** Courtesy Landesmuseum Württemberg; Peter Frankenstein, Hendrik Zwietasch. **4.5.** From Keller 1866, pl. 76, 1 and 6. **5.1.** From Hoernes 1891, p. 76 fig. 16 and pl. 10. **5.2.** From *Mitteilungen der Anthropologischen Gesellschaft in Wien* 21, 1891, pl. 9. **6.1.** From Montelius 1869, pl. 2, 7-10.12.13. **6.2.** From Engelhardt 1867, p. 21 fig. t. **7.3.** From Hughes 1859, p. 42, courtesy Special Collections and Rare Books, University of Minnesota.

Acknowledgments

Many people and institutions contributed good advice, information, publications and resources to help me in the preparation of this book, and I thank them for all of their assistance. Deborah Blake and Richard Hodges of Duckworth gave me excellent advice throughout the process. Ray Davies skilfully coordinated the transmission and improvement of the illustrations. The Department of Anthropology at the University of Minnesota helped support research trips during which I was able to collect much of the data. Other individuals who contributed with good advice, publications and other kinds of assistance were Douglas Bailey, William Beeman, Jörg Biel, Bernd Engelhardt, Lothar von Falkenhausen, Melanie Giles, Giles Guthrie, J.D. Hill, Richard Hingley, Jennifer Immich, Kristina Jennbert, Lars Larsson, Sonja Marzinzik, Vincent Megaw, Robert Murowchick, Conor Newman, Marguerite Ragnow, Nico Roymans, Peter Schröter, Jeffrey Chipps Smith, John Soderberg, Martha Tappen and Werner Zanier. The Interlibrary Loan Department of Wilson Library at the University of Minnesota was always helpful and prompt in obtaining for me bibliographic resources that our own library does not hold. My wife Joan and my sons Chris and Nick provided constant and cheerful inspiration and support, as always.

Preface

Why do so many of the images and decorative motifs that characterise early medieval brooches, belt buckles and even chalices and illuminated manuscript pages look so much like images and motifs of the Early La Tène period of a thousand years earlier? The striking similarity between these styles has long made me wonder what kind of connection could link them. We do not have evidence for direct stylistic continuity through the intervening centuries, and the societies of fifth and fourth century BC Europe and those of the sixth, seventh and eighth centuries AD were different in important ways. Could the similarities result from common ways of creating visual images, independent of any 'meaning', in the sense of specific deities, mythological creatures or heroes represented in the images?

In this book, I examine visual images from early Europe with this question in mind. In the process, I hope to suggest a new approach to understanding why people created the images and decorations that they did.

We can gain special insight into the human past if we try to understand how people created the world in which they lived, why they created it that way and how the material culture they fashioned shaped their ideas and emotions. Since its inception during the Enlightenment, the study of Europe's archaeological past has been conceived very much the way study of the natural sciences has been organised – by developing categories and by sorting objects into them. It has been an approach that has imposed a modern structure on the materials made by peoples in the past. That approach served to organise the discipline of archaeology and to provide the basic typological and chronological sequences that have been essential to the creation and development of a systematic body of data. But this approach has not included attempts to understand the people of the past in their own terms.

This book develops a framework for studying how people created their material culture to serve their own needs. The approach I take here is through study of the visuality of the past – the visual quality of manufactured objects and of created landscapes – as one way to learn about how people organised their lives. This approach depends on developing an understanding of similarities and differences between the way we see things today and the way people saw things in the past, as I outline in Chapters 2 and 3. Neuroscientists are making great advances in understanding how the human brain processes visual images, and cognitive psychologists have greatly increased our knowledge about the effects of visual environments on perception. There is every reason to think – although this idea needs to be tested – that the way humans see and respond to images has been similar, if not the same, for the past 30,000 years, since the creation of the earliest documented images. Hence, the way we see the representations of animals painted on the walls of the caves of southwestern France and northern Spain, and the faces on northern European brooches of the sixth century AD, is, on a general physiological, level, the same as the way the people who created them saw them. By analysing the way vision works in modern humans, we should be able to learn why our predecessors created the images in the ways that they did. (This point needs one qualification, which I explain below.)

However, while the physical and physiological processes of seeing have probably been quite (but not completely) constant over the past 30,000 years, the visual environments in which people see things have changed. The 'visual world', to use

James J. Gibson's phrase, in which we live is very different from the visual world of Upper Palaeolithic communities and from the visual worlds of Early Iron Age and early medieval Europeans. All of the elements of the visual world in which people grow up and in which they live directly affect the way they see. To learn how people in the past responded to the images they encountered, the best source of information we have is the contexts in which those images occur. We can study how they arranged images and other objects as decorations on their bodies, in graves, on ritual sites and in the landscape.

The one qualification to my general statement above that the visual systems of humans in the past worked similarly to ours relates to the recent findings by neuroscientists that the physical structure of the brain actually changes with the mental activity in which it engages (Chapter 2). The examples I cite involve London taxi drivers and people who meditate, but the principle should apply to any mental activity. Even among modern study subjects, this research is in its infancy, and no one, as far as I know, has attempted to investigate such changes in the past. But the issue is one that we need to bear in mind as we consider similarities and differences between they ways in which we see objects today that were made and used in the past and the ways that the people who made and interacted with them saw and responded to them.

I use a small number of specific objects or classes of objects throughout the book as examples to illustrate my points. Most of these come from 'elite' contexts, as do most of the complex images and decorations from early Europe. By 'elite' I refer to individuals and groups with greater authority, power and wealth than the majority of people, without implying anything about the specific character of the social and political systems. A comparable study of visuality of material culture associated with non-elites would be very productive, but space does not permit me to explore that topic here.

The theoretical basis of my approach derives from a number of different disciplinary fields concerned with images and our perceptions of them. I have made extensive use of the studies of James Gibson, Richard Gregory, Timothy Wilson and Melvyn Goodale and David Milner from the field of cognitive psychology. Research by Semir Zeki, Eric Kandel and V.S. Ramachandran in the field of cognitive neuroscience informs much of my interpretations of human responses to images. Early work on decoration by Alois Riegl and later studies by David Brett have been useful in thinking about how ornamental objects were designed and perceived. In the field of art history, Ernst Gombrich, Michael Baxandall, David Freedberg and Donald Preziosi have informed much of the discussion. In what I shall call 'image analysis', covering a variety of different approaches, studies by John Berger and W.J.T. Mitchell have been particularly useful.

In order to keep the text relatively free of citations, I include references to specific works only when I cite a particular page. Otherwise, the reader will find all of the relevant literature pertaining to points made in the text in the Bibliographic essay and in the Bibliography.

1

Image and response in Early Europe

Images, today and in the past

Today we are inundated with images. Every day most people who live in modern urban societies see hundreds, if not thousands, of them. The most numerous are photographs in newspapers and magazines and on the internet, and the moving images on television and in film. Museums display images in the form of paintings, photographs, sculpture and other media. Books contain photographs and drawings. We hang pictures on our walls and set them on our desks and mantelpieces.

Humans have been making images for at least the past 30,000 years, and the creation and use of images seems to be a universal, or near-universal, characteristic of human societies in recent times. But in the past, images were much less common than they are today, in our current world of mass dissemination of information and pictures. And they played different roles from those that they currently play.

Images created in the past have long served as sources of information about earlier peoples. Academic studies and popular accounts of Early Stone Age societies have regularly included photographs of Upper Palaeolithic representations, especially images from the cave paintings of France and Spain. Books dealing with historical periods frequently include images, such as photographs of statues, medieval engravings or pictures of twentieth-century battles. In the past couple of

1.1. Map showing principal sites dating between 600 BC and AD 800 mentioned in the text.

decades scholars such as Simon Schama and Peter Burke have presented critical approaches to the use of images as sources of information about past societies, even those for which we have substantial written records.

Images – of all kinds – are rich in the information they contain for our understanding of the peoples, and of the individuals, that created and used them. This book examines some of the potential information that images can yield, about one context in the past – temperate Europe between 600 BC and AD 800. This span includes what modern researchers have named the Early Iron Age, the Late Iron Age, the Roman Iron Age and the early medieval period (the latter includes what are known as the Migration period, the Dark Ages and the Merovingian period). Throughout these centuries, the production of images became increasingly common, mainly in contexts associated

14

with elites. It was a time when societies in temperate Europe were in regular contact with peoples of the Mediterranean world and thus with communities that used writing to some extent as a means of recording and communicating information. Writing had already appeared in southern France in the sixth century BC in association with Greek activity in the area around the mouth of the Rhône. By AD 800, literary culture was spreading in monastic and other church communities throughout much of northern and northwestern Europe.

Images from this period have been much studied by archaeologists, art historians and others. In this book, I take a different approach to the study of images from those in most investigations. Most researchers have approached the images from early Europe with the assumption that they look the same to us as they did to the people who made and saw them 2,000 years ago, and their analyses and interpretations have proceeded accordingly. Here I challenge this assumption and suggest other ways of thinking about, examining and understanding them. My essential question is, why did the people who created and used the images make them the way they did? Two related questions follow. How did they see and respond to them? How were their visual experiences different from ours?

Images, their meanings and what they did (and do)

Since the beginnings of systematic archaeology in Europe, images have fascinated both scholarly investigators and the public. Early finds such as the Gallehus horns (see cover illustration), the first of which turned up in 1639, spurred speculation about the meaning of such representations. As archaeology developed into a systematic discipline in the latter half of the nineteenth century, the principal focus of efforts involving many of the objects bearing images was typological and chronological. The basic frameworks for the organisation of European archaeology as a field of research were being established, and the fibulae, belt hooks, standing stone sculptures and other objects were viewed largely for what they could contribute to working out the chronological sequences.

When investigators began to make connections between images found archaeologically and European deities known from Roman accounts or from later medieval traditions of mythology, much of the figural ornament came to be interpreted in terms of religion and ritual. As the quantity of material grew during the latter half of the nineteenth and start of the twentieth centuries, the representational art of the Iron Age played a major role in discussion of influences of other artistic traditions upon those of Europe, an approach exemplified by the works of Paul Jacobsthal in the 1930s and 1940s. In the latter part of the twentieth century, as anthropological and sociological themes attracted interest, objects bearing images came to be understood as symbols of status, identity and even ethnicity. Some investigators propose that many of the objects could be best understood in terms of magic and apotropaic powers. Others, notably Lotte Hedeager, drew connections between the images and the design patterns and the formation of new political awareness in the early medieval period.

All of these approaches have been productive and have helped us to understand the complexity of image-bearing material culture in late prehistoric and early medieval Europe. My concern here is different. My focus is not to try to arrive at a 'meaning', in the sense of semiotic, symbolic, religious or political significance for the various images, but rather to understand their visuality – the visual quality of images and significance that that quality had for the people who saw them. A number of researchers have recently warned about the futility of attempts to link early images with myths, legends or religious beliefs that were recorded in later texts. For example,

1. Image and response in Early Europe

Johann Callmer notes that 'meanings' (as we would understand them) of images and representations of scenes changed substantially through time, and it is therefore very unlikely that a later written account of a religious belief, say, would correspond closely to an earlier image. Whatever the producer of an image (whether an Iron Age bronze caster or a twentieth-century painter) intended as its purpose, it is ultimately the individual viewer who perceives the image and assigns meaning to it, a point emphasised in different ways by art historian Richard Brilliant and neurologist Oliver Sacks. In this sense, I think that the pursuit of 'meaning' in prehistoric representations is highly problematic and unlikely to yield satisfying results, at least at the present state of our understanding. As Semir Zeki observes, images serve to represent in a material way ideas and narratives that were important at one point in time, but that are likely to have changed since the images were created. In cultural contexts without writing, stories, ritual procedures and other practices vary each time they are enacted. Without written guidelines to follow, the performer inevitably varies the content of the performance each time. Images represent a particular moment in the activities of makers, viewers and responders, but they cannot change with changing circumstances.

Images are objects, not just ideas, and as such, they survive materially. To appreciate their significance to the people who made, used and responded to them, we must evaluate them as actual *things* in the cultural world, as Alfred Gell reminds us. This subject is very different from the meaning of the images, in the usual sense, although there is a connection. I wish to argue that the *form* of the image is at least as important as the content with regard to how images functioned in the past, and how they function today. Whereas content depends on what the viewer brings to the image, visuality is a set of properties of the image itself.

Different ways of seeing

Comparative studies of representations of humans produced by artists and artisans in different societies show that humans, animals and other subjects can be represented in quite different ways. What a twenty-first-century Londoner might consider a realistic representation of a person might be quite different from what an individual in another time and place might consider realistic. As an exhibition on the *Human Image* at the British Museum in 2000 emphasised, there are many possible ways of representing humans, and what one person might consider realistic another would consider highly stylised.

Mary Beard and John Henderson show how our modern western ideas about portrayals of the human form (the same would apply to animals) developed from modes of representation practised first in Greece and later in Rome. They argue that Johann Joachim Winkelmann (1717-68), who played a key role in creating the fields of art history and Classical archaeology as they developed over the next couple of centuries, established the 'Classical ideal' forms of sculpture and painting by which we judge representation today. The discoveries of Roman sculpture and painting at Pompeii and Herculaneum had a major impact on thinking about these matters in Europe and America during the eighteenth and nineteenth centuries. Before Winkelmann, Giorgio Vasari (1511-74) had argued that the tradition of painting that developed in Florence during his time recreated the greatness of Classical art, and that this was the ideal of representation.

It follows from this perspective that we live in a tradition that regards the particular modes of representation that were developed and practised by sculptors and painters in Greece during its Classical period, then adopted by the Roman world several centuries later, as the ideal styles of image making. We in the modern West have grown up with the idea that the particular style that developed in those contexts, and that was revived in what we know as the 'Renaissance', is the mode of representation that is most 'realistic'. At the same time, different traditions developed in other parts of the world. Since the middle of the nineteenth century, new styles exemplified by artistic movements known as Impressionism, Expressionism, Cubism, Abstract Expressionism and Pop Art have challenged the traditional assumptions in the West.

Regarding our ideas about what a landscape should look like – whether a 'real' landscape in the outdoors or a rural scene painted by John Constable – Ann Jensen Adams makes a similar point about our current ideas deriving from a specific context in the past. She argues that our current notion of landscape derives in large measure from Dutch paintings of the seventeenth century, which set the visual standard in European styles of representation for the next three centuries. For historical reasons that she explains, the landscape in seventeenth-century Netherlands came to have a powerful cultural resonance, which is embodied in the views painted by such artists as van Goyen and van Ruisdael.

These perspectives addressed by Beard and Henderson and by Adams help us to understand that the way we see is not the way that everyone has seen. A few examples from recent studies serve to make the point that other investigators have found that close study of experiences of seeing shows that people in the past have indeed seen differently from the way we now see. In a study of pilgrims in early Christian times, Georgia Frank finds that attitudes and beliefs played a major role in what people saw and how they responded. She writes (2000: 103) that '... understanding "visuality" (defined as "the meanings, properties, or values that a given culture assigns to sight") is largely a reconstructive process, one that considered how language, symbols, myths, and values become attached to the act of seeing'. She goes on to note, 'exploring visuality in a particular cultural context requires careful attention to the poetics and organization of visual experiences'.

In his study of painting in fifteenth-century Italy, Michael Baxandall makes similar observations. While all modern humans (*Homo sapiens*) have had in the past, and currently have, essentially the same physical structure of pupil, lens, retina, nerve fibres, receptors and brain (a point that will be discussed later in Chapter 2), he argues, the way the brain operates to interpret visual images differs from person to person according to experience. Each person sees differently, depending on that person's accumulated experience of seeing and responding to images. The question then arises, how different are the visual experiences of different individuals? Surely two people raised in similar environments and with similar educations would be likely to see objects and images quite similarly, but what about two people who lived millennia apart in time and with very different surroundings and experiences? How different would their visual experiences be? And how exactly would they differ?

Changes in perceiving visually

As we shall see, vision, visuality and visual reception and response depend greatly on context. But there are also some broad changes that have greatly affected vision and visuality, and these need to be taken into account in any consideration of the differences between our visual perceptions and those of the peoples we are considering two millennia ago.

Perhaps the most important of these changes was the development of printing in the fifteenth century. Before that, the images that most people saw were relatively few in number. Certainly since the Bronze Age, elites had had access to images on jewellery, vessels and weapons, from Greek and Roman times sculpture and painting, and these arts continued into medieval times for the elites. But with the development of printing, it first became possible for much greater numbers of people (but still only a small proportion of the total population) to see and even to acquire pictures of things. While the effect on the majority of people may not have been great or immediate, the growing 'middle class' of Renaissance Europe experienced a profound change with the proliferation of images.

Another major shift came during the nineteenth century with the development of photography in the first half and that of techniques such as half-tone printing in the 1880s. Once photography became relatively inexpensive by the 1880s, huge numbers of middle class and poorer people were having portraits taken, and attitudes to images changed profoundly. The development of high-speed methods for printing fundamentally changed the reproduction of images from the relatively laborious process of manhandling the presses to the highly mechanised process that allowed for vastly greater efficiency in turning out images. Implications of this change formed the subject of one of Walter Benjamin's best-known essays, *The Work of Art in the Age of Mechanical Reproduction*. This process of an ever-greater proliferation of images reached its modern culmination with the image (re)production of Andy Warhol and television and now the internet.

The investigator's responses

Several investigators in different fields of inquiry make an important point about our attempts to understand how people in the past perceived the visual world in which they lived. We need to proceed by assessing how we see and respond to an image from the past, fully conscious of the fact that our response is probably different from theirs. Zwijnenberg and Farago argue (2003: xi-xii) that the investigator's response to a visual image must be 'an intrinsic and necessary part of scholarly investigation' and that this approach '[acknowledges] our contingent position as viewing subjects'. If our goal is to understand images from the past, we need to take into account our own way of seeing and of responding to them as a part of the images' potency. Tim Ingold makes a similar point with respect to investigating the impact of landscape on the observer. We need to assess, analyse and interpret our own visual experience before we can begin to assess the ways that people in the past may have seen and responded.

The material: images in early Europe

In later prehistoric temperate Europe, figural imagery first became relatively common in elite contexts in the second half of the Early Iron Age – during the sixth century BC. Figural imagery can be traced all the way back to sometime before 30,000 years ago, according to current dating evidence, with the earliest examples including small ivory sculptures of animals from the Hohle Fels and other cave sites in southwest Germany, and animals painted on the walls of the cave at Chauvet in south-central France (Figure 1.1). During later periods of the Upper Palaeolithic, thousands of animals were painted and engraved on the walls of caves, especially in southwest France and northern Spain, and sculpted and engraved in bone, ivory, antler and stone. Human figurines, mostly of women, were also sculpted in these materials, although rarely represented on the walls of caves. During the Neolithic period, ceramic figures of women, and a few men, were made, especially in the southeastern regions of the continent, as well as some of animals. In the Bronze Age, representations are generally less common in most parts of temperate Europe.

Images of humans and of animals first became a regular part of the material culture of individuals of above-average status during the latter half of the Early Iron Age, after 600 BC, and their appearance represents a major change in the way that people thought about themselves and about their relationships with other people and with animals. Representations occur in a number of media, including cast and hammered bronze, pottery and life-size stone sculpture.

In the Late Iron Age, about 400 BC to AD 50, personal ornaments, especially fibulae, neck rings and bracelets, bear numerous images of animals and humans. Sometimes the whole body of the animal or human is represented, sometimes just a head or face. Bronze vessels that were used in communal feasting were ornamented with figural images. In later centuries of the Late Iron Age, coins became the first mass-produced medium to bear images, with both animals and humans represented. Sword scabbards often have images of animals engraved or in relief. Other objects associated with elites also bear images, such as sheet metal horns, fittings on ornate wagons and fire-dogs (andirons). The exceptions to these were the enormous figures carved into the landscape, of which the Uffington White Horse is the best known.

In the Roman Iron Age, we find, as might be expected, somewhat different kinds of images within the Roman provinces and beyond the frontier, although with considerable overlap. In the Roman imperial lands, coins were very abundant. The great majority had a portrait of the emperor on the obverse, and a scene of political importance on the reverse. Stone and bronze sculpture was quite common, and gravestone reliefs were abundant. Small cast figures of deities were common household accoutrements and offerings at sanctuaries. Pottery was decorated with relief figures. Mosaics and wall paintings brought figural ornament into the houses of the wealthy. Military equipment, including the standards and weapons of officers, bore images of animals. Much sculpture in the Roman provinces reflected native religious ideas expressed in the Roman medium, including statues and reliefs of the goddess Epona and the mother goddesses.

Beyond the frontiers in northern and eastern parts of Europe, Roman Iron Age figural representation included many imports from the Roman world, especially coins and terra sigillata pottery, but also locally developed traditions. Examples of local use of figural imagery include friezes on bronze vessels, such as those from Himlingøje, both human and animal relief representations on sheet ornamental metalwork, such as the disks from Thorsberg, and animal-shaped fibulae such as those from the spring deposit at Bad Pyrmont. Much of the weaponry recovered in the great bog deposits in northern Europe is adorned with figural images, especially in the form of birds, but also human faces.

From the end of the Roman to the early medieval period, particularly common media for images are fibulae of different types, especially the large bow fibulae that were in common use throughout Europe between the end of the Roman period and the eighth century. They bear a number of distinctive forms of imagery, particularly birds of prey, serpents, horses' heads and human faces. Belt buckles often bear similar imagery. Weapons often bear figural images, including helmets, belt fittings and shields, and the horse harness fittings associated with weapons in graves are often decorated with figural imagery as well. Bracteates are a well-represented medium of imagery, especially in northern parts of the continent, but they are also widespread elsewhere. Gold crosses and other early Christian objects frequently bear images of religious importance. Standing sculpted stone of the later part of the early Middle Ages was also important in carrying figural images, such as the Gotland stones of Sweden and the high crosses of Ireland. The illuminated manuscripts from the eighth century onwards were an important category of figural ornament in a new medium.

All of this evidence depends on the vagaries of survival. Other than under unusually favourable conditions of preservation, and particularly careful recovery techniques, images of wood and textile rarely survive from this period. Hence my discussion focuses on metal and stone objects, because these are the best-represented materials that come down to us from these centuries.

Why did figural representation become more common in the sixth century BC? There are two different ways of thinking about this question. The traditional interpretation, ever since Paul Jacobsthal defined the field of study of Iron Age art with his 1944 *Early Celtic Art*, has been that it was contact with the Greek world that fostered the development of the tradition of figural imagery in temperate Europe during the sixth century BC. Figural imagery had been common in Mediterranean lands well before this time, and during the sixth century BC there is increasing evidence for interaction between Greece and Italy and the lands north of the Alps, mostly clearly evident in the 'southern imports' – Attic pottery and Greek and Etruscan bronze vessels on settlements such as the Heuneburg in south-west Germany and Mont Lassois in eastern France and in rich burials such as those at Hochdorf and Vix. Greek-made objects such as the bronze hydria from Grächwyl in Switzerland and the krater in the Vix burial seem to provide prototypes for bronze figures made locally.

But we now know that the matter is more complex. If it were as simple as local craft production being stimulated by objects brought in from Greece and Italy, why were borrowing of ideas and themes not more complete? For example, why did artisans take up the idea of the small cast bronze figure of a person or an animal, but not the idea of two-dimensional figures painted on Attic vessels? What is now clear, but was not so clear in Jacobsthal's time, is that societies all across the temperate zones of the eastern hemisphere, from Iberia in the west, across the whole of Europe and the Mediterranean, through the lands north of the Black Sea, as far east as China, were manufacturing small metal figurines in this period. Thus there is no need

25

to think that the artisans of temperate Europe took up the practice of casting bronze figurines from the Greek world in particular – the development was part of a much wider network of societies in interaction. The nature of these interactions and the dissemination and adoption of different styles and motifs throughout the temperate regions of Europe and Asia are themes awaiting full investigation.

The character of the visuality of the images in temperate Europe from the Early Iron Age to the end of the eighth century was strikingly consistent. The similarities over time are especially apparent if we compare an Early La Tène ornament with that of the early medieval period – the animal decoration, the stylised human faces and the curvilinear patterns. The following chapters suggest why images were created as they were, and why these particular patterns and techniques persisted over such a long period of time.

2

Vision, visuality, visual images

The subject of this chapter is how we see. The topic is immense, and I can provide only the briefest of outlines here of the points that are essential to the discussion of the evidence in Chapters 4-7. In order to begin to consider our topic – the visuality of images in early Europe – it is essential to explore some of the fundamental questions of visuality, about how people see and saw things.

Seeing is a much more complex and subtle process than most of us think. From the earliest recorded theories from the Classical period in Greece about how vision works until the early nineteenth century, a wide range of different ideas have been advanced about how light enters the eye and how the eye transmits the information it receives to the mind. These early theories of vision need not concern us here. At least since the time of Helmholtz (1821-94), researchers have appreciated that the way we see is not at all obvious. Considerable advances in the past several decades, especially in the fields of cognitive psychology and cognitive neuroscience, have greatly increased our understanding of the processes. From the work of numerous artists of the past, it is apparent that many of them understood the subtleties of how vision works, although they probably did not appreciate exactly why it works the way it does. As practising neuroscientists make clear, there are still many aspects of vision that are not yet well understood.

The physics of seeing

The purely physical (as opposed to psychological or perceptual) process of seeing begins with light passing through the front of the eye, through the pupil and through the lens, and striking the outer surface of the retina. Light stimulates the photoreceptors (each eye has about 120 million of them), and these in turn transmit information, in the form of electrical pulses, along the optic nerve, consisting of some million fibres, to two main regions in the back of the brain. V.S. Ramachandran (2004) describes one as part of an 'old system' in evolutionary terms, responsible primarily for enabling us to perceive spatial relationships. The other he calls the 'new system', and this one leads directly to the visual cortex. This visual area of the brain does the work of identifying objects.

The visual cortex has been found to consist of some 30 distinct areas, for reasons that scientists do not yet fully understand. Studies have shown that if one specialised area is damaged, others can take over the function that had been played by the damaged one. The brain is therefore much more adaptable and malleable with respect to seeing than scientists believed until recently.

Thus we do not, as some have thought in the past, see a simple projection of the outside world on our retinas, such as the projection of a film on a screen. Rather, the process of transmission of light from objects onto our retina is the first stage in a complex process of interpretation by our photoreceptors of what is out there. It is our brain that sees, not our eyes. As Semir Zeki (1999: 3) writes, 'what we see is determined as much by the organization and laws of the brain as by the physical reality of the external world'.

V.S. Ramachandran (2004) makes the important point that to fully understand both how vision works and why it works the way it does, we need to consider why it evolved as it did. He identifies two main purposes for which our vision developed – to find and recognise things – especially food and potential mates – and to spot predators. This evolutionary perspective would imply two main functions of our vision – to see and interpret things that we need for survival, and to see things that could kill us.

Cognitive psychology of vision

Conscious and unconscious vision

While the neurons of the retina send signals about light that they receive through the optic nerve to the parts of the brain responsible for interpreting them, the brain needs to work hard at sorting the information it receives. The human brain consumes around 20% of the total energy that the body expends, although it represents only about 2% of body weight. Timothy Wilson notes that every second our eyes process some 10 million signals. These are too many for the brain to consider and sort consciously; the brain can handle only some 40 bits of information in a second. Thus there are mechanisms in the brain that determine – in ways of which we are not conscious – which signals warrant conscious attention and which can be ignored. Part of the selection process depends on the brain's previous experience and stored memory. In other words, what the individual has seen and responded to before largely determines what will attract the brain's conscious attention.

In their studies, Melvyn Goodale and David Milner distinguish two different systems of vision, both of which play important roles. One is the conscious and allows us to perceive things in the world around us and to think about what we are seeing. The other, less researched and thus less well understood, is largely the unconscious. This second system of vision provides us with vital information to negotiate everyday life. An example of this second system is our visual reception of and response to traffic signals while driving. We do not think consciously about seeing a red traffic light or a car stopping in front of us – both our vision of and response to these are automatic. If we had to think consciously about everything we see and react to in everyday life, we would progress extremely slowly through our daily routine. Robert Kurson presents an informative study of a man named Mike May, who, long after a childhood accident left him blind, regained sight in middle age. May had to take considerable time to deliberate before undertaking actions that most people perform without thinking, because his system of unconscious vision-and-response was underdeveloped.

Scanning and fixation

When we look at something – that is, when our brains decide that something in our field of vision is worth devoting conscious attention to – our eyes scan the surface of the object of our attention. We sweep our eyes back and forth, focusing on one point, then shifting to another, back to the first, then to a third point, and so on. This practice is easy enough for us to experience ourselves, and it has been demonstrated experimentally many times. As the eyes sweep over the surface, our brains and eyes do three distinct but interrelated things. (1) They focus on particular aspects or parts of the subject. Experiments show that points of special interest draw the more concentrated attention of our eyes and brains than other portions of the subjects we look at. In Richard Gregory's Figure 3.16 (1997), for example, an experiment showed that the observer focused most intensely and most repeatedly on the subject's eyes in the photograph, and secondarily on the mouth and the top of the head, while sweeping across the cheeks and forehead without pause. (2) They seek out the edges, or the frame, of the subject. If the subject is a human face in front view, they trace the outline of the face. If it is a painting, they move around the edges of the canvas, along the inner edge of the frame; if a statue, then around the perimeter of the figure. (3) They strive to connect the two, to situate spatially the parts of the subject under focus within its edges. This third action is essential in creating the visual context for the subject, by literally 'framing' it within a boundary. Thus when a person focuses visual attention on an object, such as an Early Iron Age bronze vessel or a silver-and-gold fibula from an Anglo-Saxon grave, that person's eyes first scan the surface of the object, looking for edges and for the points on the surface that attract attention most intensively, then fill in the details with back-and-forth movement to relate the edges to the visual high points and to the surface between them. A modern visitor to a museum, or observer of photographs in a book, follows this same procedure, and viewers 2,000 years ago probably did likewise.

A topic of current research in cognitive psychology is the amount and quality of visual information that a person is able to gather with a rapid scan of a subject. Can a quick scanning glance provide all of the information that the brain requires to collect relevant information, or does a quick scan serve instead to inform the brain that it needs to focus for a longer time on the subject? This question has important implications for the use of visual elements on objects of material culture. For example, can a quick glance at a complex fibula provide the observer with all of the information needed to understand the information that the fibula can transmit? Or does the quick glance only inform the observer that the object is complex and requires longer and perhaps closer visual analysis?

The cognitive map

Our visual system acts creatively. Besides selecting those signals that it understands as related to things seen before and remembered, the brain creates what has been called a 'cognitive map', a model of what the world 'looks like'. This cognitive map is the essential model of the world that we have in our brains and with which we compare everything we see. Much of what we see we have seen before and can recognise immediately. Some things may be new to us, but our cognitive map may enable us to place them in a category that is familiar. Something that is completely foreign to our experience and therefore not part of our cognitive map we may not be able to identify visually.

In seeing things, interpreting what we see, and responding to our interpretations, our expectations play a vital role. The way that we perceive things depends directly on the memories built up from past visual experiences. This information is stored in the neurons and synapses in our brains. When we look at a painting, for example, most of us see more than splotches of coloured material applied to a sheet of canvas or panel of wood. Our brains have experienced images similar to paintings, and probably paintings as well, before, and we understand what we see in relation to those past experiences. With the new trends in artistic production since the end of the nineteenth century, known by names such as Impressionism, Cubism and Abstract Expressionism, professional artists have tried to challenge these ways of seeing that our societies have developed over the centuries. To someone unfamiliar with the aims of Picasso and Braque, their Cubist paintings were incomprehensible – the patterns of colour on the canvases were not part of the cognitive maps of most early twentieth-century museum goers. By now, anyone with a serious interest in painting and anyone who has taken a course in art history has some understanding of Cubism. Its patterns of representation have become parts of people's cognitive maps.

One of the special features of our dynamic visual system is our ability to create three-dimensional images from two-dimensional patterns of light hitting our retinas. We owe this ability in large measure to our experience, usually from a very early, pre-conscious age, of touching things and comparing what we see with how the objects feel. This experience, together with the brain's sorting and comparing processes, enables us to 'guess' accurately most of the time (but not always) what an object at a distance looks like, as well as how it would feel if we could touch it.

Often we are confronted with something that is not immediately familiar, and we have difficulty fitting it into our cognitive map. In a relatively dark setting, for example, an object that we would recognise immediately in daylight might look unfamiliar. When we are unable to recognise the object – to fit it into a place on our cognitive map – we can become confused and feel threatened. But often after a brief hesitation, suddenly it becomes apparent what the object is, and we can categorise it as familiar. The sensation can feel almost like a click, as the brain switches from confusion to understanding. Another everyday example that illustrates the adaptability of the brain to changing visual stimuli is the shaky vision we experience just after getting a new pair of glasses. 'Your eyes will adjust quickly' we are told, but of course it is the brain that adjusts to the new lenses. For a few hours after putting on the new glasses, the world around us looks odd and our experience of vision feels unfamiliar; usually within a day, everything seems normal again. The brain has adjusted to the changes brought about by the new lenses.

Seeing complex objects

In both learning about the world when we are infants through seeing and touching things, and processing visual information later in life, we rely especially on edges and borders of objects. The sweeping motion of our eyes across the surface of an object from edge to edge is important in the brain being able to form a full 'picture' of the object. It is extremely difficult to visually grasp an object if we make the effort to keep our eyes still, focused just on that object. The more complex the surface of an object, with patterns of decoration, curved shapes, three-dimensional features and multiple colours, the more time and attention our brain devotes to examining it and figuring out what it is – how it corresponds to our cognitive map, a point developed for early medieval fibulae by Torill Lindstrøm and Siv Kristoffersen and for modern advertisements by Margaret Livingstone.

Objects of visual complexity, as I define in Chapter 3, do not occur in nature in the same way that they have been created by humans. Except for the alterations introduced by humans, landscapes tend to be visually simple, relative to the visual complexity of human-altered environments. In any single place where a person could have stood and looked in temperate Europe during the Early Iron Age, the most visually complex elements would have been structures built by humans – stone circles and megalithic tombs, burial mounds, houses, fences, markers on some graves. Otherwise, the visual landscape was made up of fields and woodland, hills and mountains, rivers, lakes and coasts. Nearly all of these features were visually 'soft', with smooth, rounded edges, and patches of consistent colour, except where a brightly hued bird or butterfly interrupted the pattern. Burial mounds fit smoothly into the visual landscape without greatly interrupting its contours, and trees, with their foliage and their flexibility in the wind, also did not constitute hard, sharp-edged phenomena such as those created by humans. Only things like standing stones, fences and houses formed such sharply delineated interruptions in the visual landscape. Early humans did not, as far as we know, try to replicate nature (as some modern artists do), but instead emphasised the artificial aspects of what they fashioned.

Similarly, the small and portable objects in the natural world presented little of the visual complexity of many crafted items.

2. Vision, visuality, visual images

Pebbles, fallen twigs and branches, acorns and pinecones, birds' eggs, and even the mammals and birds that inhabited the temperate European landscape tend to be symmetrical in shape, smooth rather than sharp-edged, and of muted colours. Objects fashioned by humans, from chopping tools and hand-axes to elaborate early medieval belt buckles, are generally much more complex visually.

Fooling visual perceptions

Our visual perception can be fooled, as is demonstrated most clearly in optical illusions. What we see (that is, what our brain sees) depends both on the link between the visual signals received and how they compare to our cognitive map, and on what we expect to see. Numerous experiments have demonstrated that people see what they expect and do not see what they do not. For example, in an illusion that Kurson reproduces (2007: 232), a human-like creature chasing another looks bigger and its face actually seems to have a fiercer expression, even though the two figures are identical. In human experience, people being chased almost always appear frightened, while people doing the chasing appear aggressive or angry. Our brain imposes that knowledge on the scene and sees what it expects to see.

But of course our visual perception is also fooled by representations. As many cognitive psychologists observe, paintings, for example, are illusions. They are flat surfaces with colouring material applied to them, and when we look at them, we think we are seeing pictures of people, or landscapes, or whatever other subject the painter has suggested by the way the colours have been arranged.

When we are paying close attention to one visual pattern, structure or event, we can be oblivious to others, in a phenomenon known as inattentional blindness. Ernst Gombrich demonstrates this phenomenon in relation to the 'figure versus background' situation. If we concentrate our attention on one part of a visual representation, we are likely to miss another part, or the background. In an example, he cites a print that shows an ornate urn and a pair of trees. We focus our visual attention on the urn, especially its thick upper portion, and miss the message 'hidden' in the edge between the subject and the background. If we focus instead on the background, we see two profiles, one outlined by either side of the urn. They are, Gombrich tells us, of Louis the 16th of France and Marie Antoinette. If, knowing that this image hides other secrets, we look further, we discern two additional faces defined by the branches of the trees. If we did not know that we should look for hidden images in this picture, we would be unlikely to notice them. This relationship between what is represented in the foreground (where the viewer tends to focus) and the background (which is often ignored) is an important issue in the analysis of the transmission and reception of visual representations.

A different but equally striking example of inattentional blindness resulted from a now-famous experiment in which subjects were instructed to watch a videotape showing small groups of people passing a basketball back and forth. The subjects were instructed to count the number of passes. At one point in the experiment, a person wearing a gorilla costume walked through the centre of the action, in one scene even stopping to pound on its chest. As they reported their counts of the basketball passes, the subjects were asked whether they saw anything else other than the basketball players in the video. About half said that they did not and expressed surprise when they watched the video a second time. This experiment confirms numerous related experiments that demonstrate that we fail to see things that we are not looking for.

Change blindness is a related phenomenon. In experiments,

subjects are shown two pictures in succession and asked to tell what is different between the two. In an example illustrated by Gregory (1997: 47-50) showing a scene of a number of people, the colour of the hat worn by a man in the centre of the picture is different in the two illustrations. In a case shown by Chris Frith (2007: 43), two photographs show a line of people boarding a large aeroplane. In the first, the large jet engine is prominent next to the line, in the second, it has been removed from the image. Many subjects do not notice these relatively minor changes because they are not expecting them. This phenomenon has important implications for our understanding of differences between pairs of similar but not identical objects, such as the two ornate fibulae in the Cologne woman's grave (see Chapter 6).

Images shape the mind

We are accustomed to thinking of images as reflective of ideas, values and attitudes of a community, and to use them as a means of gaining insight into both their creators' and consumers' minds. But recent research has drawn attention to what Barbara Stafford calls the constitutive aspects of representations. We need to consider not only how images stimulate emotional responses, as Freedberg has documented, but also how they affect the way our brains work – how we think and how we view the world. Thus as we consider the images created by artisans in the Iron Age and early medieval Europe, we need to be aware that these images played some part in telling the people who saw them how to think, especially how to conceive the rest of the visual world in relation to the created images. Changes in the character of images, or in the ways that they are presented, should give us clues about changes in thinking.

Visual and mental experience and structural change in the brain

One of the most important recent developments in neurobiology and cognitive neuroscience is the discovery that the human brain changes its structure with experience. In the process of learning, from before birth on, our brains develop neural networks based on our experience seeing, feeling, hearing, tasting and touching. The neural networks we form encompass our brain's perception and understanding of all aspects of visual reception, as well as of the other senses. Infants and children develop their neural networks faster than adults, because their brains contain vast quantities of neurons ready to do just that. A very large proportion of each person's brain's visual perception system is formed during the first months of life.

Until quite recently, it had been thought that the structure of the brain was fixed and that it changed only through trauma, disease or the various degenerative processes associated with ageing. But studies have shown that this is not the case. The brain is much more flexible, adaptable and active than scientists had believed. Several recent studies using magnetic resonance imaging of brains show that the physical structure of the brain changes through use, with particular regions expanding or contracting according to the amount they are used. The most famous case study that dramatically illustrates this point is that of the enlarged hippocampus of London taxi drivers. The hippocampus is the part of the brain in which information about spatial patterns is stored. Brain scans of London drivers reveal hippocampus sizes significantly larger than those of other people, and apparently their hippocampuses continue to grow as they work driving around their city. In order to get their licences as taxi drivers, London taxi operators need to memorise the locations of all of the streets in London and be able to tell the most efficient way to get between any two points. Thus they need to keep an exceptional amount of spatial data in their heads, and in the course of their work, they regularly 'exercise' this portion of their memory. Another study shows that people who meditate for extended periods of time develop larger areas of portions of the cortex in their brains.

The implications of these findings are significant for all studies of visual reception and memory. They suggest that for any particular visual activity, an individual is likely to develop the part of the brain that is most directly involved to a greater extent than another person, and that therefore the individual with the experience is likely to be more effective in that visual activity than another person would be. Thus, not only is experience itself important for future visual reception and response, but the structure of the brain is actually altered to favour future success in that activity.

Development and character of visual perception

As everything said above should imply, our vision – what we see and how we respond – depends on our experience. Even before birth, developing infants have been shown to respond to light coming through their mother's abdomen. Right after birth, a baby begins to learn about the world around it through vision and touch. Through the baby's visual and tactile interaction with its environment, its brain creates the cognitive map. This map is expanded and revised throughout the individual's lifetime, but the experience of the first few months plays a disproportionate role in a person's visual system and its functioning. It is highly significant that the infant 'learns to see' by touching things in its surroundings – its mother and father, stuffed animals, the sides of its cot – and thus begins the creation of its cognitive map, long before the child develops speaking. The vital role of this very early development is underscored by the inability of people who were blind at birth ever to 'learn' to see later, even though their physical vision may be enabled later in life.

Every individual's cognitive map is unique. Each one of us sees everything at least slightly differently from everyone else. The more similar the environments in which a group of individuals are raised, the more similar will be their cognitive maps and their visual experience.

Recently, two main theories of the nature of visual perception have dominated discussion. One suggests that we perceive the visual world directly. What is out there is what we see, through the various mechanisms of the eye and the brain. The other argues that we do not have such direct perception of the physical world, but rather perception mediated by our brain, its experiences, and its memory, or, put another way, by our cognitive map. In this interpretation, instead of seeing objects directly, our brain generates inferences or hypotheses about what is there. It tests these inferences against the cognitive map that it has developed and, when necessary, alters that map according to new information coming in. Richard Gregory presents a series of examples of incompletely drawn figures. Although the lines are incomplete, our brain enables us to 'see' the total figures, because we compare what is there on paper with what we have seen before. Other examples are pointillist paintings, where close up we see only coloured dots, but from a distance we see a scene; and half-tone photographs in newspapers, which are also comprised of tiny dots, visible only with a magnifying glass.

Visual perception of images is especially complex compared to perception of everyday objects such as trees and spoons. As Oliver Sacks has shown, images are created according to culturally specific practices, and without familiarity with those practices, a person might not be able to recognise what an image was intended by its creator to represent. Furthermore,

40

as W.J.T. Mitchell and others have argued, images frequently possess a kind of life of their own and thus require a more complex set of understandings in order to appreciate them.

Visuality in the past

Since our visual system and cognitive map depend to a great extent on our early childhood experiences with vision and touch, people who lived in the distant past had different visual systems and cognitive maps, because their physical surroundings were different. Even today, studies have shown that people raised in different settings have different ways of perceiving the world visually.

Infants and children in modern industrial societies are exposed to a great many images, both three-dimensional and two-dimensional. Most children become familiar, through sight and touch, with toy stuffed animals and dolls. From early ages they see pictures in books and images on television. Most children 2,000 years ago saw very few images. Even for a context as recent as the seventeenth century in the Netherlands – a period we think of as a high point of representational art – Muizelaar and Phillips emphasise how special paintings actually were, because there were simply not very many images around. Further back in time, during the Iron Age and early medieval periods, people's visual worlds were very different from ours today.

3

Structuring visuality

Given the current theoretical understandings of how vision works (see Chapter 2), this chapter examines specific topics that will be important for applying theories of visual perception to the material evidence from early Europe.

Structures of visuality

Neuroscientists, social scientists, anthropologists and art historians studying vision, perception and reception have drawn attention to specific aspects of the visual quality of objects that are particularly significant for how we see them. They are surfaces, edges, texture, decoration, glitter, colour and lighting. Important themes include pictures, faces and shape referencing. In the process of considering these elements of visual quality and these themes, I define what I call 'visual complexity'.

Surfaces

James Gibson brought to the attention of investigators into visual perception the importance of the concept of surface. Our vision is two-dimensional, and what our eyes see are flat surfaces of different kinds. Our brains use various clues such as shading, overlap, colour differences and experience with touch to generate the three-dimensional images that we see. Gibson's theory of surfaces offers powerful analytical potential for the examination of objects, in Chapters 4-7.

3. Structuring visuality

Surfaces can be plain, flat, with little texture and with no decoration. Examples from prehistoric Europe are the top of a fibula foot bearing no ornamentation or a grassy plain with no features visible above ground and nothing breaking the line of the horizon. Our eyes, in scanning the visual environment for information, move quickly over surfaces if they are not elaborated with distinctive texture or with decoration. But surfaces offer what Gibson calls 'affordances'. Surfaces afford the possibility of decoration. While plain surfaces are just that, plain surfaces, decorated surfaces have what he calls (1980: xii) 'referential meanings' – they refer to something else. Gibson's concepts of surface and affordance provide valuable tools for thinking about the visuality of objects in early Europe.

Edges

When we sweep our eyes over an object or a landscape, our brain looks for the edges in order to establish the position, size and character of what we are looking at. Edges serve to guide our eyes over surfaces, to direct us to where we should be looking to see what is essential, and to inform us where the information-rich image or decoration terminates. Our brains want so intensely to locate edges to orient visual experience that they subconsciously create them when they are not there, as experiments have shown.

Texture

All surfaces have texture, and the texture of a surface plays a vital role in the visual reception of what is on a surface. Frequently, the second aspect of an object that we perceive after shape is texture. For a small object such as a fibula, we see quickly whether the surface is smooth or decorated with high relief. In a landscape, we grasp immediately whether the texture of the surface is rough with rocks or trees, or smooth with manicured grass or sand. Metalsmiths and landscape architects who want to create things that will seize people's attention and make them focus on an object will employ highly textured surfaces. Even if the texture is not itself the main object of attention, it will serve to draw the eye to something else.

Texture can look very different from different vantage points. For example, a building or large stone or metal monument may look highly textured from a distance, but up close the viewer may see instead flat surfaces. At the other extreme, delicately worked objects such as fibulae or ornate bronze vessels can have surfaces textured by incised lines that are so fine that the unaided human eye can barely make them out.

Decoration

Although decoration has been much studied by art historians and design theorists, the subject has received little theoretical attention in European archaeology. Yet it can tell us a great deal about the societies of early Europe. If the edge or frame guides the eye where to look, the decoration captures the brain's attention. Decoration helps us to see and to recognise familiar motifs. It informs us about what we are looking at; as Brett (2005: 62) has observed, it 'situates us in social space'. Decoration is intended to draw the attention of our brain and to hold our attention, to make us linger. We spend much more time looking at a decorated object than at an undecorated one, and the decoration can lead us to important images that otherwise might not attract our attention.

In our modern commercial world, we have little say about how the products we buy are decorated, although of course we can choose what to buy. In pre-industrial societies, where things were made by hand, often to individual taste, all decoration was chosen consciously. It is part of what Brett (2005: 6) calls 'visual ideology'. Decoration provides a link between us as observers and the material world in which we live, move and interact. The varieties of decoration employed within a society provide observers with important clues as to what they are seeing, what else they should be looking for and how what they are observing fits into the social space that they inhabit.

Glitter

The sparkle, or shininess, of an object can be an important aspect of attracting visual attention. Objects such as the Donzdorf fibulae (see Chapter 4), with their shiny gold and silver portions and their sparkling red garnet insets, and the Sutton Hoo belt buckle, with its brilliant gold interlace pattern highlighted by niello effects, dazzle viewers who see them in bright light, whether direct sunlight or the light of a large fire. We can appreciate something of the effect of glitter on attracting and holding visual attention from the way that Rembrandt and his contemporaries applied substantial dabs of bright yellow or white paint onto parts of their paintings that they wanted to catch and guide the eye, such as gold buttons and other ornaments on portraits of distinguished citizens. This effect is well displayed in brightly lit cases in jewellery shops that emphasise the glitter of gold, silver and the stones set into them.

Colour

In all societies, specific colours have important cultural meanings. In our own, for example, red means danger and stop. Green means go at a traffic light, and good ecology in an advertisement. While we often tend to think of prehistoric times as drab, accumulating evidence shows that the Iron Age peoples used many bright colours, at least for elite members of societies. The problem is that colours rarely preserve well. The coral inlay in jewellery and ornamental bronze vessels has faded from bright red to chalky white. Textiles recovered in contexts where they do survive show that red and blue were common colours, as we shall see below. In the early medieval period, many fibulae and belt buckles and other ornaments include bright gold, silver, red garnet, blue glass and other colours. Even many of the stone sculptures were once colourfully painted, although today we see only the natural colour of the stone from which the images were carved.

Lighting

The way we see objects depends on how they are lighted, and changes in lighting greatly affect how they appear. We must bear in mind that we live in a world with copious amounts of artificial light, and we can produce light of many different kinds in order to illuminate our environments day or night. But our visual system evolved on the basis of natural light, mainly from the sun. In the absence of indicators to the contrary, our brains assume that objects are lighted from above – the natural position of the sun – rather than from below or from the side, as experiments have demonstrated.

In early Europe, all artificial illumination was created by the use of open fires – hearths in homes and halls, torches, tapers, candles and oil lamps. Except for the dim fires that must have burned in most fireplaces, the majority of people had little access to artificial light. Oil and candles were costly and could only be consumed by the elite. Even in the most lavish courts, such as those at places like Gudme in Denmark and Yeavering in northern Britain, the intensity of fire-produced light could not have come close to matching that available in the typical living room of today. The quality difference between artificial light then and now is also important in thinking about visuality. Fires flicker, and the light they emit can cause objects to appear to move.

In the process of examining a number of early medieval fibulae, I have moved a focused beam of a small torch across the surface of the objects, from different directions and at different angles, and the effect is always striking. The complex arrangement of three-dimensional ornaments makes them appear to move as the beam of the torch sweeps across the surfaces. A torch beam is not the same as an open fire, but this exercise suggests that the objects were perceived by observers of the time differently from the way we typically see them in evenly illuminated museum cases or in photographs in books.

Objects are lit not only directly by sources such as the sun and fire, but also by ambient light that is reflected by surfaces. The character of ambient light in any situation is determined by the nature of the surfaces. Objects made to be visually powerful, such as the most elaborate fibulae, belt buckles and bronze vessels, create their own means of directing ambient light. Every curve, bulbous protrusion, patch of deeply incised lines and piece of coloured inlay creates its own pattern of shadows and colour distinctions, as does every feature carved into a wooden figure or a sculpted stone statue.

Finally, there is a direct and important connection between lighting and movement. Three different kinds of movement play important roles – that of the source of light, that of the observed object and that of the observer. For visuality in landscapes, the movement of the sun is of vital importance. A stone statue will look different in the early morning, at noon and in the light of the setting sun, and seasonal differences will be significant, with the angle of sunlight changing throughout the year. On a smaller scale, a candle or oil lamp carried by a person as he or she observes an object will create special visual effects as that light source moves, as I found with my torch.

When a person wearing an ornate fibula or carrying a highly decorated jug walks across a lighted room, that motion of the object greatly affects their appearance in special ways. The principal changes that occur with movement are in the shifting patterns of areas of observed objects that are highlighted, and of areas that fall into shadow. These movements can create the impression that the objects are alive.

Themes

Pictures

This book is a study of images – of representations of humans and animals – in early Europe. But what are images or pictures, and how do they work? These apparently simple and straightforward questions are in reality extremely complex. Many philosophers, psychologists, art historians and cultural critics have grappled with the problem. The psychologist Gibson makes the important point that a picture (and the same applies to all of the images considered below) is not what we might think it is – a representation of an actual thing. Instead, it is a surface that has been manipulated in such a way that physical traces on it make our brain think of certain things that are different from the representation itself. Gibson (1986: 272) defines a picture as 'a surface so treated that it makes available an optic array of arrested structures with underlying invariants of structure'. He goes on to say (1986: 282) that 'a picture is both a surface in its own right and a display of information about something else'.

For Mitchell (2005), a theorist of images, pictures are 'complex assemblages of virtual, material, and symbolic elements'. They serve to create our visual worlds, to give us information about the natural and social environments in which we live and to connect us with the world around us.

3. Structuring visuality

3.1. Gilded silver fibula from Chessel Down, Isle of Wight, UK. Note the numerous faces that immediately attract our attention.

Faces

Human faces play a special role in the study of vision and visuality, and they will turn up in all of the following chapters (see Figure 3.1). They are so important for several interrelated reasons. In evolution, they became the part of the body by which individuals could be most easily distinguished from one another. Although there are some eight billion people in the world, we can still identify our parents, siblings, children and friends by the distinctive features of their faces. Newborn babies first become connected visually with their mothers' faces, and this early link plays an essential role in the development of ability to recognise faces in the individual's subsequent experience.

Charles Darwin was much concerned with faces, and in his *The Expression of the Emotions in Man and Animals*, published in 1872, he concluded that seven specific emotions are expressed universally in human societies with the same facial expressions. (There have been challenges to this thesis, but in general it has held up well.) Faces are extremely important not only for our identifying particular individuals but, because we know – consciously or subconsciously – the meaning of different facial expressions, they can warn us of approaching danger or assure us of friendly intentions. We examine people's faces to learn about their character as well as about their emotions, and we respond to images of human faces more intensely than we do to any other kind of image.

Shape referencing

Shapes that we recognise as representing something we know – a human figure or familiar animal – are often transformed into shapes that look something like the recognisable one, but abstracted. Instances of this pattern suggest the importance of a visual code that was known at the time, perhaps to just some individuals in a community and not to others. An example is the inverted drop-shaped bird head with long pointed beak and two round eyes that appears on decorative attachments on sword scabbards in the bog finds in northern Europe. In some cases, the bird head is clear, with the distinct eyes (sometimes of blue glass) peering out at us, as on sword attachments from Vimose in Denmark (see Figure 3.2). Very similar bird heads with long pointed beaks and round bulbous eyes occur prominently on the shield boss from Gommern in Sachsen-Anhalt in Germany. In other cases, attachments have on them shapes similar to the bird heads, but without the eyes, and sometime the beak is greatly reduced in size, as on a belt buckle and belt attachment from Vimose.

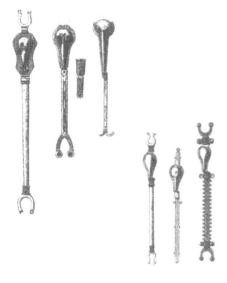

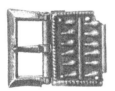

3.2. *Top:* three bronze scabbard fittings from Vimose, Denmark, with clearly represented birds' heads with eyes (in some cases of inlaid blue glass) and long pointed beaks. *Middle:* three such fittings from Thorsberg, Germany, with beaks represented but not eyes. *Bottom:* two bronze belt fittings from Vimose, with the shape of birds' heads indicated, but neither eyes nor distinct beaks.

The bird of prey head was a motif of immense importance from the middle part of the pre-Roman Iron Age onwards, and it appears on a variety of objects, including weapons, personal ornaments and coins (see Figure 3.3). When just the general form appears, without details such as eyes, as on the Vimose belt attachments, does that refer to the theme 'bird of prey'? Why were the (to us) distinctive elements – the eyes and the well-defined beak – omitted? Was some extra significance added by creating just the outline, without the details? Is this some kind of subtle and possibly thus more powerful use of the visual theme 'bird head'?

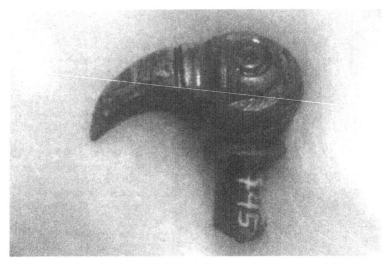

3.3. Bronze vulture head from Kelheim in Bavaria, Germany. Length from tip of beak to back of head 1.75cm.

Visual complexity

By visual complexity, I mean the quality of presenting the observer with an image or design that combines several of the structures of visuality discussed above in such a way as to powerfully, even emotionally, engage, or, to use Gell's term (1992, 1998), to enchant the viewer. A visually complex object is likely to have well-defined edges, to be highly textured and perhaps three-dimensional, to include several striking colours, to glitter, and to be intricately decorated with images, including especially faces. Among the objects discussed in the following chapters, the fibulae from Donzdorf, the Sutton Hoo buckle and the jugs from Basse-Yutz, are examples of visually complex objects.

Enhancing visuality

People who are concerned with making their images work, in the sense of forcing viewers to give conscious attention to what they see, to focus and to respond to images, use a variety of techniques to enhance the visuality of the images. Today the most familiar example is in the work of advertisers to force potential consumers to pay attention to advertisements, whether on billboards on the roads, pictures in the newspaper or advertisements on television or the internet. The techniques modern advertisers use to make people shift from their unconscious sweep through the images around them to focus on a picture and to think about it are similar to the techniques used by Rembrandt and other Renaissance painters, makers of fibulae in the sixth century and crafters of Early Iron Age belt plates.

In late prehistoric and early medieval times, craft workers practised a number of techniques designed specifically for visual effects, all of which added to the visual complexity of the objects they made and decorated. These are beyond the casting, hammering and otherwise shaping of their products. They are physical features added to the works specifically to enhance the visual complexity of the pieces.

In the Early Iron Age, hammered relief ornament and incised patterns of lines were important techniques of visually enhancing metal objects, and incised decoration was common on fine pottery. Inlay of coral and of shell was used, both on bronze and on ceramics. In the Early La Tène period, human and animal figures and faces were often represented with bulging eyes and bulbous noses, grabbing much more attention than the simpler Early Iron Age figures, and they were enhanced by fine incised lines that add texture, shading and general complexity to the images. In the latter part of the Roman Iron Age, the technique known as chip-carving (*Kerbschnitt*) became widespread for the ornamentation of belt fittings and other equipment. This method created a very three-dimensional appearance by first casting a pattern of ridges and grooves, then further shaping the grooves with a burin. The result was a highly textured surface with numerous facets that caught the light and gleamed or sparkled. This technique is well represented in the metalwork associated with weapons and with fibulae in the great bog deposits in northern Europe from the third century AD onwards.

During late Roman and early medieval times, inlay of garnet and of coloured glass came into wide use as a means of visually enhancing ornamental objects such as the Donzdorf fibulae and the Apahida 2 and Sutton Hoo purse lids. Niello involved cutting into the metal and introducing a mixture of sulphur, copper and silver to produce, after being heated and fused, black inlay in silver or gold. This technique was used to stunning effect on the Donzdorf fibulae and on the Sutton Hoo buckle. Techniques for producing three-dimensional effects were important in late Roman and early medieval contexts. In granulation and filigree, tiny gold balls or gold wires were attached to surfaces such as those on large fibulae and on precious vessels, such as the Ardagh Chalice. Cast appliqué figures created powerful three-dimensional effects on objects such as the Gallehus horns (see the cover illustration).

These were among the principal techniques that were used by metalsmiths in Early Europe to heighten the visuality of objects, in order to capture and hold the attention of observers.

Encounters

A person's encounter with an image involves a number of identifiable stages, which might be called glancing, seeing, looking, gazing, receiving, reacting and responding. Most of what goes by our eyes in the course of a day we do not even register consciously (Chapter 2) – we simply cannot, or our brains would be overwhelmed with the information content of the images around us. Once something strikes us as worthy of our conscious attention, we focus our brain on the object and 'look' at it. A split second's consideration may tell us that it merits no further attention, or it may inform us that the thing is of interest, at which point we 'gaze' – we focus for a closer, more considered examination. All of this happens in a fraction of a second. At this point, our brains begin to receive information from the object of our attention, and in response to this reception, we react. We might react with emotion – happiness or sadness – or we might react with the acquisition of information – we learn something from what we see. If our reaction is sufficiently powerful, then we may respond to the sight. Our response may be emotional, or we may make a decision, or we may take action in some way. In this sense, we can say that the image has agency – it causes people to act. David Freedberg has explored these issues, especially with respect to people's reactions and responses to Renaissance and early modern art.

Alfred Gell developed the concept of 'technology of enchantment' – the creation of images and ornament so captivating to the viewer that they 'enchant' – they fascinate, mesmerise the observer. His principal example is elaborately ornate prows of boats in Polynesia, but the concept is applicable to many other contexts. Some of the ornate fibulae discussed below, with their numerous tiny faces, hidden creatures and sparkling polychromy, are visually enchanting. Howard Williams (2006: 141) suggests that outfitted graves, with their often elaborately ornamented objects arranged in particular ways, can be regarded as 'technologies of enchantment' (see Chapter 5).

Some of the images considered below are puzzles. Many items of bronze and gold jewellery crafted in the Early La Tène period bear images of creatures with some human features and some characteristics of different animals. What were they meant to represent? Are they humans with some animal traits, or are they monsters made up of elements of different creatures? Complex fibulae of the early medieval period, such as those from Donzdorf Grave 78 and Bifrons Grave 41, and the belt buckle in Saint-Denis Grave 49, pose the question, how many faces are there? The fibula pair in the Cologne woman's grave (see Chapter 6) is a special case, in that a whole series of animals seem to be hidden in the design. Images with complex intertwined ornament, such as the Sutton Hoo belt buckle and the carpet pages of the Lindisfarne Gospels, are puzzles. Which head is connected to which foot, the viewer asks?

Why do these puzzles exist at all? V.S. Ramachandran (2004) argues that humans like puzzles for evolutionary reasons. Our ancestors of several million years ago depended for their survival on solving visual puzzles, such as identifying predators that might be hiding in the thick foliage of the African jungles and grasslands. They had to be able to spot the difference between leaves and leopards, for example. Since the ability to solve such visual puzzles played such a crucial role in human evolution (otherwise we would not be here thinking about it), Ramachandran believes, we instinctively take pleasure in confronting and working to solve visual puzzles. Children enjoy picture puzzles in which they search for 'hidden' faces or figures, and *Where's Waldo?* was a best-selling book.

The visual world of early Europeans

What we see depends to a very great extent on what we have learned to see (see Chapter 2). Neuroscientists have established that in the first few months of an infant's life, the child's brain rapidly develops the synapses – the connections between neurons – that form the basis for all perception later in life. These processes continue throughout the individual's childhood and adulthood, but at ever-slower rates. In the experience of the infant, those early explorations of vision, touch and other senses, and the knowledge and experience that build up in the infant's brain, affect *how* that individual sees things throughout life.

3. Structuring visuality

In our attempt to get closer to understanding what the visual world of Iron Age and early medieval Europeans was like, we need to think about the visual world in which infants and children lived. ('Visual world' is a concept developed by James Gibson [1950: 26], and it is 'the familiar, ordinary scene of daily life'.) To put it simply, the visual world of an infant in sixth-century BC temperate Europe was very different from the visual world of children in the modern industrial West.

In a typical middle-class residence in the modern world, an infant spends much time on a mattress in a cot, napping. When the infant is awake, there are usually one or more stuffed animals close by, and the child develops an early attachment with one of these. These are objects that the child touches and sees, and they play a highly significant role in the development of the child's sense of the world. The stuffed animal is typically big, compared to the baby, of a single colour, and soft and fuzzy.

Around the edges of the cot are bars to keep the child from rolling off onto the floor. These, together with the stuffed animals, are probably the objects that play the greatest part in the child's brain's developing senses of sight and touch. The bars surrounding the cot are very different from the stuffed animal. They are hard instead of soft, stationary instead of portable, and they present a regular, geometrical configuration rather than an irregular, soft lump. With these two things that the child sees and touches daily, the child begins to develop its sense of the appearance and feel of the world.

Most parents offer their child a great deal more visual stimulation. Suspended above the cot may be colourful shapes of some sort, and attached to the cot railing may be bright plastic discs or other ornaments. When the infant is taken out of the cot, there may be colourful plastic blocks, picture books to be looked at on the lap of a parent, and rooms full of objects of different sizes, shapes and textures.

It is useful to reflect on the differences between such twenty-first-century indoor environments and house interiors of Early Iron Age Europe. From excavations of the remains of Iron Age houses all over Europe, we can get a reasonably good idea of what interiors looked like. (A useful photograph of a house interior at the reconstructed Iron Age settlement at Lejre in Denmark can be found in Kreuz 2002: 75, fig. 47.) Iron Age houses would have been much darker than houses in our world. People probably went to bed when it got dark and arose when it started to get light. Glass windows did not exist in Iron Age Europe, so that even when it was light outside, the interior of houses would not have been bright.

Brightly coloured objects were rare in most households – they were the prerogative of the elite. Gold and silver jewellery, red coral inlay in bronze ornaments, later red enamel and garnet, rich blue, yellow and red textiles all seem to have been almost exclusively restricted to elite contexts. The same is true of colourful ceramics, such as those of the Alb-Salem group in southwest Germany.

Visually complex objects were also restricted to elite consumption. Reconstructed house interiors, such as that from Lejre cited above, show domestic environments characterised by objects that are monochromatic or at most bichromatic, most of them with smooth, round surfaces (pots, supports for a spinning wheel, stones as seats and to form fireplaces, logs for supports of houses and shelves). There is no reason why infants in the Iron Age would not have had some equivalent of our stuffed animals, perhaps something like the 'corn dollies' of British folk tradition. But more visually intricate, complex objects, analogous to televisions and music playing systems with their various screens, dials and numbers; or clocks, lamps, photographs in frames, shelves of books and mantelpieces with ornaments – all of these and many other items that form the visual complexity of our living environment today – were missing.

These considerations imply that the brains of infants in Iron

Age Europe developed their cognitive maps differently from the way our brains do today. If this is true, then we would expect people of that earlier period to see things differently from the way we do.

From the ways that objects bearing visual complexity were used – especially the burial contexts in which we find them – we can get some idea of how people 2,000 years ago responded to seeing objects differently from the way we do today. Such objects consistently occur in the wealthiest burial assemblages (Hochdorf, Vix, Cologne, Saint-Denis, Sutton Hoo), and they were clearly worn in the most visually powerful places on the people with whom they were subsequently buried. For example, in the Hochdorf burial, all of the gold ornaments on the man's body, the couch, cauldron, drinking horns and wagon, are visually complex objects. Colour also played an important role in these visual displays, often presented in bright textiles that wrapped bodies, individual objects and sometimes large parts of the burial chambers themselves (as at Hochdorf and Sutton Hoo).

The special significance of the assemblages that contain these visually complex objects is apparent when we compare them with other burial assemblages of the same cultural contexts. Many cemeteries of the latter half of the sixth century BC have been excavated in the part of Europe where Hochdorf is situated. Visually complex objects are very rare in, if not totally absent from, the great majority of graves. Many graves contain no objects at all, others contain very modest amounts of pottery, small bronze ornaments and occasional weapons such as spearheads. From this contrast, it is apparent that the visually complex objects in the rich graves such as Hochdorf and Vix had a visual power for those societies far exceeding anything we can imagine today, given our wide exposure to visual objects and images of all kinds.

Many exceptionally rich graves have yielded evidence of the use of textiles for covering objects in the burials. It seems that part of the funeral ceremony involved ritually covering objects and thereby removing them from the gaze of the participants in the ceremony. The experience of seeing objects such as the huge bronze cauldron in the Hochdorf grave being covered with bright blue and yellow textiles must have had a strong impact on the participants in the ceremony. Perhaps this removal from sight of the special, visually complex objects, even prior to them being buried in the ground, had a powerful emotional effect on the viewers, with the removal from sight of the sparkling, colourful objects that were emblematic of the individual with whom they were associated.

Leaving aside the special aspects of visually complex objects, even relatively simple figurines were restricted to a small group of wealthy burials. With figural representation in small-scale format, such as the little horse-and-rider figures impressed into the Hochdorf neck ring, the question arises, who would have been able to get close enough to the object to see these fine details? All of the richest graves, such as Hochdorf and Sutton Hoo, have large numbers of figural images in them, and the size varies widely. For example, while the tiny horse-and-rider figures on the Hochdorf neck ring require close examination to discern the form, the eight figures supporting the couch and the three lions on the cauldron could all be seen by anyone, from a distance away. This varied scaling of images suggests that there was some kind of 'visual privilege', whereby some members of the community were permitted to see figures from a distance and others were allowed to view objects up close to examine details.

Some responses to images from early Europe

As noted above, a number of researchers have argued recently that the investigator needs to assess his/her own reaction to visual images as part of any thorough study of past images and their effects. In that spirit, I briefly describe my responses to four figurally ornamented objects that I examined recently.

When I most recently saw the Hochdorf cauldron (see Chapter 5), even though I had seen it several times before, I was surprised by its enormous size. My first thought was that it was on the same scale as the Vix krater – that is, vastly out of proportion to all the other vessels in Iron Age burials. Even the lions on the rim of the cauldron seemed huge, as did the handles and attachments. All nine of the drinking horns are also unexpectedly large, and the iron one is enormous. Given that these ornate vessels strike us today as disproportionately large, the people who participated in feasts and the funeral rituals in which they played active roles must have been visually awed. Here the reaction of the modern observer is particularly relevant to assessing the likely visual impact of these vessels, because the size of objects cannot be communicated well in illustrations or in lists of measurements. The experience of standing next to the cauldron and the horns is emotional as well as intellectual – one *feels* the size of these vessels as being far out of proportion to what was needed for serving beverages (and of course that was the point). As we experience directly the appearance of these objects, it becomes much easier to imagine what participants in feasts 2,500 years ago must have felt than we could possibly do from photographs and descriptions.

The gold and garnet ornaments from Apahida Grave 2 and other burials containing related materials are most striking for their brightness, their three-dimensionality, the strongly contrasting colours and the highly detailed lines on their surfaces. Photographs cannot convey the thickness, the sense of bulk and chunkiness, of the objects, nor the glitter that emanates from the gold or from the garnet insets. In the exhibition cases where I saw them, they were lighted with intense spotlights that provided an impression of how these objects would look in direct sunlight.

When I studied the fibula from Bifrons Grave 41, the most striking visual aspect was the difference between human and animal faces that were immediately recognisable and much less distinct forms that required considerable concentration, and imagination, to discern. The maker of this object created images on two levels – images that anyone could identify quickly, and those that are difficult to decipher (at least for this observer). Perhaps part of the point was for people to see and understand that something was there that they could not fully grasp.

In close examination of the Bifrons fibula, I was struck by how different the object looked from the detailed drawing in Haseloff's *Die germanische Tierornamentik der Völkerwanderungszeit* (1981, vol. 1: 47, fig. 25). The drawing may constitute the best two-dimensional representation possible of a complex relief object such as this, but the differences were striking. The round face shown on the bow is much more life-like than the drawing suggests. As I moved the beam of my torch across the surface of this face, it seemed almost alive in the shifting patterns of light and shadow. In the middle of the head of the fibula, what appears in the drawing as a very highly stylised face of uncertain character looks much more like a distinctly human face on the actual object.

The most striking aspect of the Sutton Hoo buckle was its gleam and its three-dimensionality. Photographs cannot convey the tremendous glitter of the gold in bright light, nor the striking contrast created by the black niello dots and extremely fine lines that ornament the serpents' bodies. Also striking is the unexpected thickness of the object and the high relief of the interlaced bands.

In the case of all four of these objects (and most of the others treated in this book), the most striking sense I experienced seeing them up close was a feeling of connection with the physical objects that I do not feel when looking at a photograph or a drawing in a book. Such illustrations can serve to document the basic character of an object – its shape, colour and the nature of its decoration. But these objects, and particularly the imagery they bear, generate emotional responses even in researchers who approach them objectively and dispassionately. (Such emotional reactions are the point of Zwijnenberg and Farago's [2003] injunction to researchers that they need to assess their own responses.) The size of the Hochdorf cauldron and its lions, the colour and form of the bird heads on the attachments from Apahida, the gleam and chunkiness of the Sutton Hoo buckle and the faces on the Bifrons fibula all stimulate a sense of awe. Most striking of all are the faces on the Bifrons fibula and on other objects. They seem to be looking directly at the observer, and their apparent lack of expression makes them all the more captivating. You cannot help but wonder, who or what is that, and what is the creature behind that face thinking?

4

Images for individuals

A large proportion of objects crafted and arranged for visual purposes were designed to be worn or carried by individuals. Their purpose was to attract the attention of observers through the mechanisms discussed in Chapter 3. The examples below illustrate different aspects of these visual properties.

Ornaments worn on the body

Belt plates

Belt plates (German *Gürtelbleche* or *Blechgürtel*) are relatively common in Early Iron Age burials (see Figure 4.1). They are typically found at the waist, many still have hooks attached and on some, remains of leather belts survive. Their position at the centre of the front of the body is important for their visual function – this is one of the most effective places for display (see Figure 4.2). Bronze belt plates occur in both richly outfitted and modestly equipped burials, suggesting that their use was

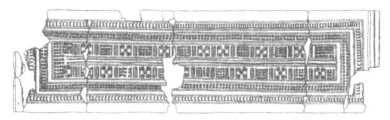

4.1. Bronze belt plate from Amondans, Doubs, France.

4. Images for individuals

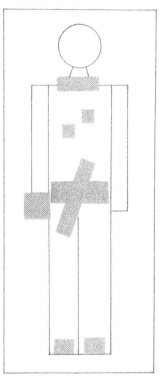

4.2. Model of the arrangement of eye-catching gold ornaments on the body of the man buried at Hochdorf, near Stuttgart in southwestern Germany. The ornaments, from the top, are the neck ring, two fibulae, the dagger, the belt plate, the bracelet on the right wrist and the sheet gold pieces on the shoes.

relatively widespread in Early Iron Age communities. They are found in graves of both women and men. Their form and size make them visually very different from other objects that commonly occur in Early Iron Age graves, such as bracelets, fibulae, knives and pottery. As flat and relatively large objects, they provide ideal surfaces, in Gibson's sense (see Chapter 3), for decoration and, with their strictly rectangular form and the clearly delineated borders of ornament on them, they have well-defined edges. Some smaller ones in particular are plain, but the majority bear complex decoration, usually executed by hammering from the back, creating highly textured surfaces on the front.

Size and ornament vary on the belt plates. Many are modest

in size, around 20cm long by 6cm wide, but others are much larger and bear complex patterns of ornament. Some are as big as 40cm long and 15cm wide, much too big to be worn comfortably. While the smaller ones may have been worn in everyday life, the large ones can only have been worn at times when the wearer did not need to move about. For the largest belt plates, we should consider the possibility that they were made specifically for the burial ceremony.

The decorated belt plates bear linear ornament in a wide variety of configurations. No two are alike. Some have repeating patterns of hammered dots, some have more complex patterns of dots, squares and circles. Some include very small figures, such as humans, horses and stags, and sometimes combinations of humans and animals. Visually, the most striking aspect of these objects is the dividing of space through horizontal and vertical lines and the filling of the defined spaces with ornament, as in Figure 4.1. The visual effect is to draw the eye in, to attract and hold the attention of the viewer, until he or she feels satisfied that he or she understands the pattern displayed.

In the great majority of the graves in which belt plates have been recovered, they are the visually most complex objects in the assemblages.

Hochdorf: gold ornaments and bright clothes

The Early Iron Age burial at Hochdorf (about 540 BC) near Stuttgart in southwest Germany provides an exceptional opportunity to address the questions posed in this book. The grave contained an abundance of visually complex objects, and, unlike the majority of rich graves of its period, it was not looted in antiquity. Furthermore, Jörg Biel's excavation of the site was a model of precise technique.

The grave was inside an oak chamber that was covered with

4. Images for individuals

a mound of some 7,000 cubic metres of earth, and it contained the body of a man about 45 years of age. He had been placed on a couch made of sheet bronze, the back of which was decorated with repoussé ornament, and it was supported by eight cast bronze figures of women. Arranged around the interior wall of the burial chamber were a variety of feasting vessels (see Chapter 5).

The man was lavishly covered with gold ornaments (the grave contained about 600g of gold). These include a decorated ring of gold around his neck, two gold fibulae on his chest, a gold belt plate at his waist, a dagger with a gold-covered hilt in a gold-covered sheath, a gold bracelet on his right wrist and sheet gold ornaments on his feet (see Figure 4.2). It is noteworthy that most of the gold objects are very thin, providing a maximum amount of surface for display relative to the quantity of gold consumed in making the ornaments.

The belt plate links his burial with many hundreds of others that contained sheet bronze belt plates, but the gold makes this one different. The two gold fibulae are of a type – *Schlangenfibel* or 'snake fibula' – common in bronze in western central Europe. The forms of the belt plate and the fibulae indicate that he belonged to the local Early Iron Age society. The gold neck ring connects this grave with about 50 others known in the region, all in graves that were more richly outfitted than the majority. This gold ring bears images in the form of tiny horse-and-rider figures, two rows of which occur around the circumference of the object. From a distance, an observer can see only that the ring is textured. One needs to be very close to discern the figures. All of the other gold objects are decorated with geometrical motifs in relief, but not with figural images.

All of the gold objects are situated in places on the body where they would be most readily seen by an observer. The neck, chest and belt regions are sites where people in most societies display ornaments that they use to communicate information.

The face – both of a live person and in a portrait or other

representation – is the most important part of the body for the communication of both information and emotion (see Chapter 3). When we look at a person, and when we converse with someone, we look mainly at that person's face. The region around the face is the ideal place to situate objects that are intended to attract visual attention, such as neck rings or earrings. Looking at someone's face allows one to see ornaments on the chest at the same time. Much of the gold ornamentation of the man buried at Hochdorf can be understood in relation to the importance of the face in presentation of the person.

The upper half of the body is also an important region of the body in another way. If we understand the torso as a surface in Gibson's sense, it becomes apparent why this is such a crucial place for display. The clothed human torso (evidence of jewellery and textile remains indicates that bodies were ordinarily clothed in inhumation burials in early Europe) offers a relatively flat surface, blank except for the texture and colour of the cloth. It offers 'affordances' in Gibson's terminology – possibilities of situating important objects for the purpose of communicating information visually. In the Hochdorf case, the surface of the torso has been decorated with a series of visually potent objects – the neck ring at the top, extending down over the top of the chest; the two gold fibulae around the middle of the chest; the gold belt plate forming the lower edge of the surface; and the dagger cutting across that edge, partly on the torso surface and partly below it. The torso is thus framed by the gold neck ring at the top and the gold belt plate at the bottom. The wide gold bracelet is situated at about the same height as the belt plate.

Similar positioning of objects is common to burials throughout the prehistoric Iron Age, the Roman Iron Age and the early medieval period. The principal field for personal decoration lies between the middle of the face and the waist, a region that comprises about 50 per cent of the body's length. In contrast, if we examine the surface provided by garments that cover the legs, we find a very different situation. Ordinarily, there are no ornaments between the belt and the feet. The feet, at the bottom edge of the body surface, are sometimes decorated with ornaments that form a lower frame of the display, as with the Hochdorf man and his gold-adorned shoes.

During exploration of the tumulus in which this rich grave was found, the excavators uncovered a deposit of tools and metalworking debris. It included remnants of both bronze- and gold-working. These smithing remains raise the question, were some of the objects made at the site of the burial, specifically for the funerary ceremony? The question does not affect the principal issue here – the visual display of ornaments on the person of this individual – but it would be interesting to know whether such items were worn during the lifetimes of such elites, or crafted only at the time of burial.

The exceptionally careful excavations and unusually good conditions of preservation led to the identification of considerable organic material in the grave, including textiles in which the man was clothed and wrapped and others that decorated the chamber itself. The man was clothed in a purple tunic, and his body wrapped in two large and ornate textiles, one red and the other red-and-blue checked. Most of the textiles had ornamental bands along their edges, framing the display of colour. (Chapter 5 will include more discussion of the Hochdorf textiles in relation to the funerary ritual.)

Glauberg fibula

One of the bronze fibulae from Grave 1 at the Glauberg is a good representative of a group of 'chunky' Early La Tène fibulae with three-dimensional, rounded features, that is significantly different in character both from fibulae of the earlier period (such as those at Hochdorf) and from the majority of fibulae of the La

Tène period, which are dominated by flat or wire forms. Although the man in this grave also wore a gold neck ring with figural decoration on it, this fibula was probably the visually most captivating object with which he was adorned. (The fibula is most captivating to me, but of course we must be cautious about assuming that Iron Age observers responded the same way that we do.) Its visually powerful qualities are based on three aspects – the extraordinary three-dimensionality, with shapes appearing as though they are jumping out at the viewer; the rich detailing of incised lines covering much of the surfaces; and the striking figures – a stylised human head and a stylised horse head as the dominant figures facing each other, and a pair of opposing dog figures at the spring end of the fibula. The fibula is 6.4cm long, and it has coral beads at either end of the iron axle.

The arrangement of the (to us) strange-looking figures suggests a visual puzzle. What is the human head with its huge bulbous nose and wildly bulging eyes doing on the back of the horse-like animal? The striking three-dimensionality of the object, and the way in which the creatures are represented, give it a playful, entertaining quality, and this effect is heightened by the red coral beads on the axle.

When the body-surface model (see Figure 4.2) is applied to Glauberg Grave 1, we find the same pattern as that at Hochdorf. This time, the shield breaks the belt border, as the dagger did in Hochdorf. Again the personal ornaments are concentrated in the upper half of the body, and there is nothing (except the lower half of the shield) between the belt and the modest ornaments on the feet.

Weiskirchen belt hook

The observer's eye immediately focuses on the large central figural element on this object, the 'Celtic style' human face, with its characteristic almond-shaped eyes set horizontally, scrolling eyebrows and moustache. As the eye scans the entire belt hook, the viewer sees on either side of the central face two figures of animals. Those next to the central element face away with their bodies, but twist their heads back toward the face; those at the edges of the object have their bodies turned toward the face, but their heads twisted in the opposite direction. The visual subordination of the animals – not real animals, but monstrous mixtures of birds, sphinxes and deer, perhaps – is heightened by the placement of the central face on a raised platform. The two animals closest to the face, whose hindquarters actually touch the cheeks of the face, have their forelimbs on the lower level, and the two outer animals have all four of their limbs on that level. Another device to draw the viewer's attention to the central face is its elaborate framing by two S-scrolls on top, the hindquarters of the two animals on the sides, and the platform at the bottom.

On the front of the platform are complex patterns of inlaid coral, including floral elements and circles. At the base is a row of small rectangular pieces of inset coral. Like all bronze, this object was shiny reddish-gold in colour when new, and the inlaid coral was bright red.

Many different photographs and at least one detailed drawing of the Weiskirchen belt hook have been published, and this object offers a good example of how different kinds of lighting affect how an object looks. We can get from this exercise a sense of the very different ways that visually potent objects appeared to people, depending on the specific conditions of lighting under which they saw them.

The colour photograph published in the catalogue of the Glauberg exhibit (Frey 2002c: 176, fig. 144) makes the relief stand out much more sharply than do the black-and-white photographs in Wells (1980: 106, fig. 5.2) and Megaw and Megaw (1989: 66, fig. 65). The central face, with its bulging almond eyes and strong chin, is more dominant in the colour photograph – our eyes focus much more intently on this central image in the colour version than in either of the two black-and-white pictures. In the black-and-white image in Wells (1980) the creatures on the sides attract as much visual attention as the central face. Similarly, in the photograph in Jacobsthal (1934, plate 7), a dark shadow under the left side of the central face changes the shape of the face, and the animals, especially those on the right, are more prominent than in other photographs. In the colour photograph, the four side animals are very much peripheral to what seems to be the central point of the image. Also in this colour photograph, the decorative patterns underneath the figural images assume a reduced visual role compared to the two black-and-white photographs. In Megaw (1970, plate 62), the lighting has the effect of showing the coral inlay in the base as equally important visually as the figures above. In the drawing in Haffner (1976, plate 14, 5), the illustrator has not used much shading, and while the central face dominates the image, the four animals look almost equally striking visually.

I use this example to illustrate that what we see when we look at the objects depends a great deal on the particular lighting conditions at the time. We cannot see the objects in their original contexts, as the people for whom they were made did, but we can at least, when we study the actual objects closely, experiment with light coming from different directions and by moving our eyes and head to get differently lighted views.

Chessel Down fibula

This object (see Figure 3.1 in Chapter 3), made of silver and gilded, provides an example of how the distance from which we see an object affects the way we perceive it. At 13.7cm long, it is a sizeable personal ornament, and from tens of metres away, its basic shape is apparent. At a distance of 10 metres, its texture becomes apparent; the observer becomes aware that its surface is not a flat sheet of metal but bears features in relief. This is approximately the distance at which individuals enter one another's social space (in modern Europe) and begin to look intensively for signs about the identity of one another. At a distance of about two metres, the three circles on the foot become evident, but it is not clear that two of them contain faces until the viewer is about 1.5 metres distant. The observer needs to be even closer, around 0.75 metres, to distinguish all of the faces on the brooch, and needs to look carefully to see them all.

As with all of the objects discussed in this chapter, the fibula has been crafted in such a way as to catch the eye, raise curiosity in the viewer and demand that the viewer approach to examine the details close up. Even from a distance of just inches away, the fibula still presents a complex array of both identifiable and not-so-identifiable images. Near the bottom of the foot is a face with scrolling eyebrows and moustache that is very similar to Early La Tène faces in style, and other distinct human faces are in the two circles on the sides of the foot. Slightly less distinct faces, but still recognisable as human, are situated at the base of the bow and on the head plate just above the bow. Along the sides of the foot are what appear to be animal heads, but of creatures not immediately recognisable (at least to me). One pair look like horses, another like snakes, a third perhaps bird heads. On the head plate are forms that seem to represent parts of animals, but they are difficult to link with any specific creatures.

This relation between distance from an object and perception of details is significant and informs us of some of the uses to which these objects were put (see Chapter 8).

4.3. Gilded silver fibula, inset with garnets, from Donzdorf in southwestern Germany. Length 13.9cm.

Donzdorf fibulae

The two fibulae of the Donzdorf pair (see Figure 4.3) exemplify the concept of visual complexity defined above (see Chapter 3). These nearly identical objects are 13.9cm long. They are made of silver, gilded and with inlaid settings of garnet. Ornamental fields are separated from one another by ridges of silver deco-

74

rated in the niello technique. At first glance, one is struck by four visual aspects of the objects – their complexity, their size, their glitter and their polychromatic colour.

Their visual complexity is immediately apparent in the variety of shapes – the rectangular structure of the head, the relatively thin but highly textured bow, and the roughly triangular foot. The head is dominated by rectangles. Its ornamental field is divided by ridges bearing tiny niello dots into three rectangular zones. Inset into the middle zone are garnets cut into rectangular shapes – seven originally on each fibula. The foot, in contrast, is dominated by completely different shapes – circles and curves. The two circles on the sides of the foot and the near-circle (actually an oval) at the tip jump out at the viewer, as do the curvilinear stylised animal heads that connect the bow with the foot. Three of the five inset garnets on the foot were circular, the other two triangular. The bow is very much a connecting link, with scrolling patterns along the sides creating an illusion of motion between head and foot, and the whole bow is dominated by a great silver cross, itself given three-dimensionality by numerous tiny niello dots and five larger dots at the centre.

The Donzdorf fibulae are among the best examples of visual complexity luring the viewer to get closer, to see in more detail what is going on in the intricate detail. After scanning the whole object, the viewer focuses on individual elements, first on the faces. Eight faces are clearest – the three human faces in the circles and oval on the foot, a human face just above the oval at the end of the foot, a human face at the foot end of the bow, two horse-like heads that join the foot with the bow and the upside-down human face on the middle of the head.

Once you as the viewer have identified the eight distinct faces, you see that there are other creatures in the patterns, which are not as readily identifiable. These include animal heads and legs in the outer rectangle of the fibula head. In the four corners of the middle rectangle are highly stylised human-like faces. An inventory of the different ornamental details on each Donzdorf fibula would include clearly defined human faces; less distinct faces that are probably human; animal heads; animal limbs, some readily recognisable and others less so; the wave pattern on the bow; the cross on the bow; niello dots on the silver ridges; figure 8s and S patterns in very fine gold filigree; and garnet inlay in gold settings.

The visual contrast between the strictly geometrical head, with its several concentric layers of shape-reinforcing rectangles, and the un-geometric foot is striking. The head form seems easy to grasp, visually, but closer inspection reveals the complex detail within the different rectangular zones. The foot is a great maze of complexity, with three-dimensional structure, openwork, four colours (silver, gold, red garnet, black niello), and ambiguous creatures and parts thereof.

These two fibulae were found in a richly outfitted woman's grave, together with other items indicative of special status, dating to the mid-sixth century AD.

Sutton Hoo belt buckle

The Sutton Hoo belt buckle catches the observer's attention first through its glitter. Of the objects considered in this chapter, it shares with the Hochdorf ornaments the sheer visual quantity of gold, unmixed with any other material except the niello lines and dots that serve to accentuate the gold sheen. Along with the visual qualities of gold, the size of this object draws the observer's gaze. As the viewer gets closer, the deep relief and the very delicately crafted lines and dots filled with niello create a finely textured appearance. When the observer is close enough to discern the pattern in the ornament, the complex array of intertwined creatures becomes visible. While the great majority of belt buckles and hooks from the Iron Age and the early medieval period are regular in shape – rectangular or oval – the Sutton Hoo belt buckle has irregular edges, determined not by a pre-set frame of the object, but by the rich decoration applied to it. The design drives the shape, adding considerable visual power to the object as a whole.

Besides the gleaming quality of the gold, the viewer's attention is caught by the complex pattern of interwoven creatures, by the contrasting colours of gold and niello, by the heads of the animals, and by the three-dimensionality of the whole design pattern. The eye is drawn to one particular point – the intertwined bodies at the centre of the object, which is in the middle of the triangle formed by the three large round raised bosses. The whole ornamental surface seems designed to pull the gaze to this one complex knot in the centre, where the viewer is confronted with a visual puzzle. Are these knotted strands all part of the same serpent, or are they different animals? How many animals are there? The captivated viewer asks, can I trace the different creatures here and follow each one separately from head to end, or will tracing the design lead nowhere? The maker of the Sutton Hoo belt buckle created this part of the design as a puzzle to intrigue and to fascinate anyone drawn into its pattern.

Saint-Denis Grave 49 (Arnegunde)

Grave 49 excavated underneath the cathedral of Saint-Denis near Paris contained the skeletal remains of a woman about 45 years old, richly adorned in personal ornaments and colourful textiles, with a gold ring on her left thumb that was inscribed with the name ARNEGVNDIS and the word REGINE. Arnegunde is known to history as wife of the Frankish King Chlothar (511-61), and mother of Chilperic. Her burial probably took place between 565 and 570.

Two main topics are of special interest here – the use of

colour and the arrangement of objects in the burial. The textiles recovered in the grave are of special significance, because they were unusually well preserved and provide valuable information about the display. On her body she wore a silk violet tunic, and over this was a broad belt with a highly ornate and complex buckle. Over the tunic was a long robe of bright red silk. Around the wrists of the robe were bands of red satin with intricate patterns of gold thread sewn into them. Over the robe was a cape of darker red colour, and a veil. The first visual impression of an observer would have been of bright colourful surfaces covering the woman's body.

These surfaces were adorned with jewellery. At her head were two gold earrings decorated with filigree, and two small gold pins holding the red satin veil. A great silver pin decorated with gold and garnet held her garments at the left side of her chest, while a pair gold-and-garnet disc fibulae held her garments at the front, one situated at her neck, the other at the waist. An unusually large and ornate belt buckle and its counter-piece, made of gold and silver, inlaid with garnet, and highlighted with niello patterns, was at her waist. The buckle itself is divided into 11 areas, each one decorated with one or two garnets and with minute filigree in figure-8 and other curling patterns. These zones are bounded by thick silver borders in high relief, with tiny niello dots along the centre of the lines. Two serpent or dragon heads with open mouths mark the end away from the tongue of the buckle. The base of the tongue is divided into three zones filled with filigree lines, and the tongue terminates in an animal head. The loop around the tongue is divided by silver borders into four gold zones, each with complex filigree patterns in them. The counter-piece is almost identical to the buckle. Besides the serpent/dragon heads, both buckle and counter-piece have several other apparent heads formed in the silver relief work, but they are much less defined, and one cannot be sure that they really are heads.

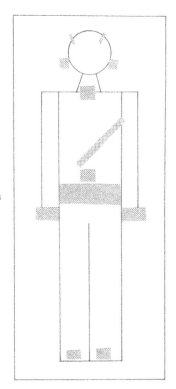

4.4. Model of the arrangement of eye-catching gold, silver and garnet ornaments on the body of the woman buried in Grave 49 at Saint-Denis near Paris. They are, from the top, two hair pins, two earrings, a disc fibula, the silver pin across the chest, a second disc fibula, the two belt fittings, embroidered gold cuffs on each sleeve and buckles on the shoes. (Fittings on the lower legs are not shown here, because they were covered by textiles and would not have been visible to participants at the funeral ceremony.)

Numerous silver strap-ends, some of them gilded, and some with ornament of bird heads and boars, adorned smaller belts and fasteners.

This grave is strikingly similar to Hochdorf in the way that images and colours were displayed. Just as in Hochdorf, the Saint-Denis arrangement called attention to the face, torso, waist, wrist and feet (see Figure 4.4). Where Hochdorf had the gold neck ring to accentuate the face, Saint-Denis had gold earrings and pins. Hochdorf had two gold fibulae on the chest, Saint-Denis had the silver, gold and garnet pin. Both individuals were buried with large and ornate belt attachments. Where Hochdorf had a large gold bracelet, Saint-Denis had elaborate embroidery of gold thread on the sleeves of her tunic. While both had gold ornaments on the feet, the visual emphasis in both burials was on the upper half of the body.

Carrying ornaments

Some ornaments displayed by individuals are neither worn directly on the person nor on the clothing. I consider just two examples here: Iron Age scabbards and Migration period harness and riding equipment.

La Tène period sword scabbards

The upper ends of bronze or iron scabbards from Late Iron Age sites such as La Tène in Switzerland frequently bear images (see Figure 4.5). The ornament is most often in the form of incised linear patterns, but sometimes appears in relief. Many specimens bear figural images, especially opposed creatures facing each another, often serpents or dragons, or birds of prey.

4.5. Ornaments at the tops of two iron sword scabbards from La Tène, Switzerland.

4. Images for individuals

The character of these images is an important indication of their intended purpose in eliciting responses. In contrast to the objects discussed in the first part of this chapter, these images are for the most part visually simple, often no more than single lines forming stylised representations of animals or designs. They were structured in such a way that their content could be grasped quickly. Unlike the Hochdorf gold neck ring and the Donzdorf fibulae, the viewer is not drawn to approach these images for a closer look – everything is there in simple two dimensions for immediate comprehension. The simple image conveys information about the owner of the sword.

Apahida 2 horse-riding equipment

Personal ornaments in richly outfitted burials of the fifth century AD in eastern Europe are characterised by their brilliant colours and by the bird-of-prey motif. In Apahida Grave 2, in the Transylvania region of Romania, many objects that formed parts of horse gear were associated with the buried individual. Among these ornaments were two images of eagles, thought to have decorated a wooden saddle, and 27 ornaments that include the heads of birds of prey.

The two eagles, 11.5cm long, are made of gold. The entire surface of the bodies is covered with cells that are filled mostly with small plaques of garnet, but in a few places – the edges of the wings and the face – of green glass. These are eye-catching devices. The 27 smaller ornaments – all 3.8cm wide – are made of iron, gold, garnet and green glass. On two sides of each are stylised heads of birds of prey, inlaid with garnet.

These ornaments are comparable to the La Tène scabbard decorations in that they are visually not complex, and thus the visual content can be absorbed quickly. The animal figures are not ambiguous, nor does texture create visual complexity that requires concentrated examination. These images, like those on the scabbards, were intended to be understood quickly.

Reshaping the body

In addition to ornamenting themselves with crafted objects that they wear attached to their bodies (such as earrings and bracelets) or fastened onto their clothing (fibulae and belt hooks and buckles), humans practise a range of ways of artificially shaping their bodies, from filing their teeth to binding their feet to keep them from growing. The most prevalent type of body shaping in temperate Europe during the period of concern here was shaping of the head, a practice well documented during the fourth, fifth and sixth centuries AD in regions of eastern Europe but with many examples in cemeteries as far west as France.

The shaping was achieved by binding the person's skull when he or she was an infant and the skull was still relatively soft. The result in most cases is a skull that is longer than average, in some cases almost conical and coming to a rounded point at the back. This practice is most often associated with eastern European groups, such as those known as Sarmatians, Huns, Alans, Goths and Gepids, and it is abundantly represented in cemeteries north of the Black Sea and eastward into central Asia. It is not clear whether the examples in cemeteries in western parts of Europe are skulls of individuals who themselves moved from eastern Europe westward, or local people whose parents decided to shape the heads of their children.

Such shaping of the body differs fundamentally from decorating it by the wearing of clothing or jewellery in that it is irreversible. An individual cannot change the shape of his or her head in adulthood. The visually most striking effect of cranial shaping is the long, conical form of the skull, but the process of binding also affects the shape of the face. People with such altered heads must have appeared distinctive and visually striking, especially in regions in which the great majority did not have such shaped body parts.

A less permanent means of shaping the body was through manipulating the hair. Unlike shaped skulls, hair does not usually survive in archaeological contexts, but it is clear from a number of finds, such as among the bog bodies of northern Europe, that some groups created distinctive hair arrangements. Different ways of treating the hair have been observed, including shaving half of the head and tying long hair into a pattern known as the 'Swebian knot', so called after Tacitus' reference to a distinctive hair fashion among one group of the people he called 'Germans'. Although we have too few examples of preserved hair to say much about exactly how hairstyles were used to create particular visual appearances, we can say from the evidence of the bog bodies that much effort was devoted to shaping the hair in particular ways. Four bronze heads bearing the 'Swebian knot' ornament a bronze basin recovered in the rich burial at Mušov in Moravia, attesting to the significance of the hairstyle as a device for communication and representation.

Indirect evidence for the role of shaping the body for its appearance comes from the abundance of toilet implements, especially in the Late Iron Age through the early medieval period. J.D. Hill has demonstrated a significant increase in the occurrence of tweezers and nail trimmers in the final century BC in Britain, a sign that more attention was being devoted to personal appearance at that time. For the Roman period in Britain as well, Crummy and Eckardt have documented continuation of this practice of ritual disposal of toilet implements used to fashion particular visual aspects of the body. This frequent occurrence of implements for creating an image of the body in burials from the Late Iron Age on raises important questions not just about why these concerns should have developed at this time, but also why they should be part of grave assemblages. Whatever the reasons, their presence tells us that personal appearance was important enough that the tools for maintaining it belonged in the final statement of the individual's personhood.

5

Images for the group

Many objects ornamented with images were intended for use by groups rather than by individuals. The social interactions between members of the groups were important components of the visual functions of the objects (see Chapter 8). This chapter focuses on the use of visual images on two main categories of objects: vessels and coins. Vessels include pottery containers and the metal vessels that are restricted to elite contexts. Both kinds were used in sets for the consumption of food and drink, an activity that occurred in family units or other social groups, although the direct evidence for such group consumption is forthcoming only in elite contexts. Some of the more richly outfitted burials contain elaborate sets of vessels, many bearing decorative imagery, that inform us about feasting practices. Coins provide a different perspective on visual culture.

Coins first became common in temperate Europe during the second century BC, when silver and bronze coins came into regular use to complement the gold coinage that had begun earlier. The expansion of coin minting, which was carried out at most if not all of the *oppidum* sites and at many smaller settlements, was the first mass-production of images in temperate Europe. Before that, every image, and every object that bore an image, was crafted individually. With the coin die, a great many virtually identical images could be produced and disseminated.

Vessels: pottery and communal consumption

The most abundant material that was shared by groups of people throughout the Iron Age and the early medieval period was pottery. Although in burials pottery is associated with individuals, its use was in social situations, in the preparation and consumption of food. While fibulae and belt fastenings were worn by individuals, and their visual qualities pertained to them, the visual characteristics of pottery referred to the group that used it.

Much Iron Age and early medieval pottery was visually plain, bearing little surface decoration and no second colour. But much pottery bore ornament that was visually significant. In the Early Iron Age, geometrical patterns were characteristic, incised and painted, and in some regions multiple colours decorated pottery, as in the Alb-Salem ceramics in southwest Germany. Elsewhere, as in the Oberpfalz in northern Bavaria and around Sopron in western Hungary, figural decoration was added to some Iron Age pottery.

On many large vessels bearing geometrical ornament from graves in the Early Iron Age cemeteries at Sopron, scenes show highly stylised representations of humans and animals. On the example here (Figure 5.1), five figures shown as filled triangles incised into the surface of the ceramic have arms, legs and tiny heads. Two are engaged in what appear to be spinning and weaving. A third figure may be processing textile materials or possibly playing a harp. Two others have their arms raised in a gesture commonly associated with adoration.

Our concern is not with the 'interpretation' of the scene, but with noting the visual impact of this figural representation. The figures are on the lower part of the neck and on the shoulder of the vessel, the part most visible to an observer looking at the vessel horizontally or slightly downward from a higher position.

5. Images for the group

5.1. *Above:* ceramic vessel from a grave at Sopron, western Hungary; height 43cm. *Below:* the scene represented by incised lines on the neck and shoulder of the vessel.

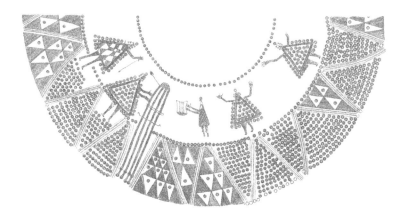

Since they extend around the whole of the vessel, the observer would need to either walk around the vessel or turn the vessel to see all of the figures. Thus the visual reception of the scene requires physical interaction with the object, which creates a relationship of direct involvement between observer and image. We do not know whether this vessel and others bearing similar kinds of images were made expressly for burial, or whether they were used in food consumption earlier. Both food consumption and funerary ceremony are communal activities. Groups of people saw, became visually involved and interacted with these scenes, at least in the funerary ceremony if not also before.

Feasts and funerals

Many of the objects that bear decoration of images were made for use in feasting, a ritual activity of great importance socially and politically. Sources as diverse as the Greek accounts of *symposia* by Plato and Xenophon, Tacitus' remarks (*Germania* 22) on drinking ritual among the early Germans and *Beowulf* provide accounts of feasts that share significant features in common.

Sharing of food and drink in a ritual setting is near universal among human societies. For Europe we have copious evidence about the structure and the importance of the feast, from the early accounts cited above to modern banquets. Common to most feasts is the display of particular vessels used for holding liquids, serving and consuming beverages such as wine, beer and mead.

For Iron Age Europe, we have several sources of information about how feasts were performed and what objects were involved. One is pictorial representations of feasts in the Greek and Etruscan worlds, cultural contexts with which elites of temperate Europe had active contact during the sixth and fifth centuries BC. Within temperate Europe, a number of bronze

5.2. Feasting scene on the situla from Kuffarn, northeastern Austria, showing two servers, a celebrant and rows of situlae hanging from hooks.

vessels ornamented in the style known as Situla Art bear scenes of feasts (Figure 5.2), providing views into the ceremonial activities of elite groups. Such feasts are represented in many well outfitted graves, such as that at Hochdorf.

Hochdorf and its feasting assemblage

At the man's feet in the grave at Hochdorf was a bronze cauldron made in a Greek workshop and on top of it a bowl hammered from sheet gold. Across the chamber from the man, on the east side, was a four-wheeled wagon loaded with nine bronze bowls, three bronze basins and implements thought to be associated with slaughter and cooking of livestock, namely an axe, a large knife, a point fashioned from a deer antler and an iron spit for roasting meat. On the south wall of the chamber were hung nine drinking horns, eight aurochs' horns with bronze and gold trim, and one, substantially larger than the others, of forged iron with broad gold bands decorating it (Figure 5.3). The reconstruction drawing in Biel (1985: 48-9) gives a good impression of the visual configuration that a person attending the funerary ceremony for this man would have seen. The size of the chamber and the amount

89

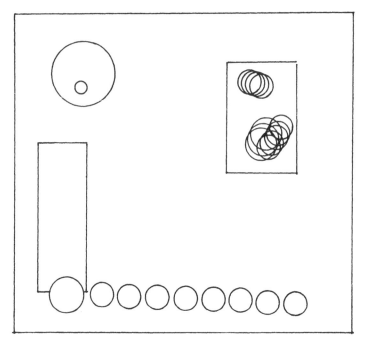

5.3. Schematic plan showing the arrangement of feasting vessels (circles) in the grave at Hochdorf, and their spatial relationships to other furniture in the burial (rectangles). The nine circles in the row along the south wall of the chamber are the drinking horns, eight made from aurochs' horns and one larger, iron horn. The large circle at the upper left is the enormous cauldron, with the small gold bowl set on its rim. The overlapping circles in the rectangle at the upper right are the three bronze basins (larger circles) and the nine bronze plates, arranged in two stacks on the wagon. The long rectangle at the lower left represents the couch. Note how the feasting vessels are arranged in such a way that they surround the open space in the centre of the chamber.

of space devoted to each part of the assemblage in the burial is striking.

The size of many of the objects that made up the feasting set was the visually most striking aspect. The cauldron is enormous, with a diameter of 1.04 metres, height of 80cm, and capacity of 500 litres, much larger in reality than it appears in any reproduced images. Its nearly spherical shape further emphasises its size. The iron drinking horn also seems disproportionately large – 1.23 metres long, with mouth diameter of 14.5cm. With these dimensions, it is difficult to imagine how it could have been used to drink liquid. At this scale, its purpose was certainly for display – to convey the idea of enormity – of the vessel, and perhaps hence of the status of the man with whom it was buried. At its pointed end, the great iron horn had a protome in the form of a bull's head, a shape reference perhaps to the idea of horn and perhaps to the wider theme of bull's heads in Early Iron Age Europe. Even the eight aurochs' horns were much larger than what we might imagine as a heroic portion of liquor. This set of outsized vessels was certainly designed and arranged in the grave to create profound visual images of the funeral ceremony that would remain vivid memories for long after the event.

The other vessels in the grave are of more modest size, conforming to the scale of objects in other graves of the period. The gold bowl that had been placed on the rim of the cauldron was 13.4cm in diameter and weighed 72g. The nine bronze bowls on the wagon ranged from 27-32cm in diameter and the three basins were around 44cm in diameter.

The undisturbed Hochdorf grave provides a special view into the public visual aspects of Early Iron Age feasting, and it corresponds closely to the feasting scenes in the Situla Art. The great cauldron with its decoration of three recumbent lions and the nine great drinking horns were designed and arranged to create images of enormity (and thus of power). None of these objects would have been used by a single person; all were accoutrements of group feasting. The rich figural ornamentation on the bronze couch similarly had a mainly social role rather than an individual one. The repoussé decoration on the back, showing sword-dancers (or sword-fighters) and sword-wielders on wagons, was designed to be viewed from the back when someone was sitting on the couch or, when the couch was unoccupied, from the front as well. A scene on the Certosa situla shows two people sitting on a couch about the same size as the Hochdorf couch. The eight figures holding the couch would have been visible to all observers, even from some distance away (the four figures on the front are 35cm tall, those on the back 32cm). It is likely that the couch and the cauldron were meant to act together in feasting rituals hosted by the chief, and that their figural ornamentation was part of a single visual complex.

In the final stages of the funerary ceremony represented at Hochdorf, colourful textiles played important parts. As noted in Chapter 4, the man buried in the grave was dressed and wrapped in several colourful fabrics. Textiles were also arranged on the couch under the man, they were hung on the walls of the chamber and they were used to wrap all of the objects in the grave before the chamber was closed. Textiles as visual surfaces have a wide range of meanings, but I focus on just two in connection with Hochdorf. In her analysis of the Hochdorf fabrics, Joanna Banck notes that the most highly ornamental of all the textiles in the grave – she calls them 'masterpieces' – were draped over the cauldron. This action of placing the most highly decorative of all of the textiles on that object during the ritual would have had the effect of drawing observers' attention to that particular object. We can only speculate why that might have been done. As an object that represented the man's role as host, as leader who presented feasts to his followers, was this the most important object from the perspective of those conducting the ceremony?

The final act in the burial chamber was to wrap all of the objects – the cauldron, the drinking horns, the man and the couch, the wagon with its bowls and basins – in textiles. This performance can be understood as a means of assuring that the individual objects and the ceremony would long remain in the memories of the people who observed the ritual – what better way to make a lasting visual impression than to remove fascinating objects from sight during the performance of a ritual?

The Basse-Yutz jugs

The two bronze jugs from Basse-Yutz are among the visually most elaborate and stunning objects of feasting equipment from early Europe. Like a number of other bronze jugs (such as those from the Dürrnberg and from the Glauberg), the general shape of these nearly identical vessels was adapted from the Etruscan jugs known as *Schnabelkannen* that were imported in substantial numbers into temperate Europe and buried in elite graves between about 500 and 400 BC. The Basse-Yutz vessels were found together with two *stamnoi* of Etruscan manufacture. These four vessels were most likely part of a feasting set from a richly outfitted burial of this period, but unfortunately the find circumstances are unclear.

With heights of 40cm, the modest size of these vessels is noteworthy, compared to the very large vessels in the Hochdorf burial. None of the many rich burials associated with ornaments of the Early La Tène style contains such enormous vessels as those in some of the earlier graves, such as those at Hochdorf and at Vix. This change has important implications for how funerary rituals were conducted and how participants experienced them.

The rims, spouts, handles and bases of these jugs are highly decorated with visual elements, while the main part of the bodies were left as smooth, polished surfaces. At first glance, the viewer's attention is captured by the three-dimensional figures clustered at the rim – the dog-like creature that serves as the top of the handle and whose head dominates the scene, and the two recumbent dog-like animals on either side of the opening. Everything about their construction emphasises their three-dimensional quality and acts to hold the gaze of the observer. The enormous pointed ears are thrust upward. On the ears and on the limbs are large spirals executed in high relief, and all along the lines of the ears, the brows and the limbs are tiny incised dots. Deep hatching with incised lines gives the bodies texture. Spirals along the back of the creature that forms the handle adds to the fascination of these creatures. The tiny ducks that sit (or are they swimming?) at the far ends of the spouts are much more realistically portrayed, with none of the ornamental spirals or other attention-grabbing devices of the 'dogs'. At the base of each handle is a classic Early La Tène face, with huge round, coral-filled eyes, scrolling eyebrows, curved moustache and 'palmette crown' above the head. These faces are ornamented much like the 'dogs' on the rim, with dense stippling along the outside and on the brows, and with high relief spirals around the face and terminating the brows.

These jugs were highly colourful. Bands of coral inlay draw attention to the base part of the jugs, and coral is inlaid in a band around the rim, on the top of the spout and underneath the spout on the front of the neck.

These two jugs are fascinating, in every sense of the word. While the initial response to them is heightened visual interest and an intense desire to get closer, to look around the figures to see what is there, the longer one gazes, the more one is fascinated by the relationships between the four animals on the top and the La Tène face at the handle base. The detailed ornament is important in drawing the attention of the observer ever closer to the piece.

Sutton Hoo feasting

Mound 1 at Sutton Hoo contained a burial that was placed in the ground about 1,150 years after that of Hochdorf, on the coast of East Anglia in England. The composition and arrangement of objects suggest visual functions strikingly similar to those of the Early Iron Age grave near the centre of the continent.

Both were situated under large mounds of earth constructed in such as way as to be visible from some distance away – they were monuments in their respective landscapes. The structures of the burial chambers differed. At Sutton Hoo, the burial chamber was built inside a 27 metre long seaworthy ship that had been hauled from the water and buried in a trench. As at Hochdorf, the chamber contained a variety of special objects distributed along the walls and across the interior.

Unlike the situation at Hochdorf, at Sutton Hoo no skeletal remains were found with personal ornaments arranged as they had been at the time of the funeral ceremony. Instead, at Sutton Hoo they were placed into containers that removed them from the sight of participants in the ceremony. As at Hochdorf, in the Sutton Hoo burial we can identify three main categories of objects that pertain to different aspects of the man buried. First were objects that informed observers about his status. These included the gold belt buckle, the purse with its ornate lid and the shoulder clasps. The second category was the man's role as a warrior, represented by the sword with its ornaments, the helmet, the highly decorated shield, the spears and the 'standard'. Third, and of special concern here, were the objects that attested to his role as host of feasts – the great cauldron, the hanging bowls, the Anastasius dish, the 10 silver bowls, the buckets and bottles, ladles, spoons and drinking horns, as well as the lyre.

As at Hochdorf, at Sutton Hoo feasting vessels were spread out in the burial, not packed together in one part (Figure 5.4). This pattern in both graves suggests that the visual presentation of the man's role as host was an important part of the funerary ceremony. Many vessels were arranged along the east wall of the chamber. The great silver dish, a small silver dish, the drinking horns and the wooden bottles were placed between

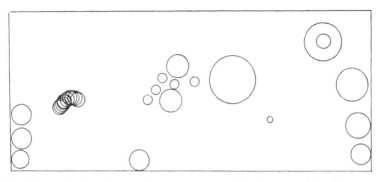

5.4. Schematic plan showing the arrangement of feasting vessels in the chamber of the grave in Mound 1 at Sutton Hoo. As with the Hochdorf chamber, note the arrangement of vessels throughout much of the burial space, in this case along both west and east walls and in the centre of the open area. (For details on the individual vessels see plans in Bruce-Mitford 1972 and Carver 1998 and 2005.)

the east wall and the middle of the chamber. The 10 silver bowls were arranged closer to the west wall. The feasting vessels of Sutton Hoo were more evenly spread over the chamber than were those in the Hochdorf grave.

Several authors have recently emphasised the *performance* of the funerary ceremony at Sutton Hoo, with a series of visually impressive stages. The hauling of the boat, the digging of the trench to accommodate it and the building of the wooden chamber were all visually powerful actions that people performed in and to the landscape. While we do not know the exact sequence of the events in the funeral, the arrangement of objects can provide useful information. Howard Williams emphasises the importance of the colourful textiles and of the glittery gold and garnet objects in creating a visually enchanting atmosphere. He describes (2006: 140) an 'animated scene, flickering light in which gold and silver objects ... textiles would appear to shimmer and move'. Among the textiles, he notes the colour reference between the red and yellow textiles and the red of garnet and yellow of gold in the metal ornaments.

5. Images for the group

At Sutton Hoo, as at Hochdorf, an important part of the ritual process was covering objects, making them no longer visible to participants. Personal ornaments of the man at Sutton Hoo were placed in boxes, presumably after they were displayed to the observers. Vessels and weapons were wrapped in cloth before they were arranged in their places in the chamber.

Mass production of images:
Iron Age coins

Investigators of Iron Age coinage have emphasised the use of coins as money, and their proliferation from the middle of the second century BC has been understood in the context of other changes that were taking place at the time, such as increasing interactions with the Roman world and emergence of an urban-type civilisation based at the *oppida*. Colin Haselgrove and David Wigg-Wolf challenge that approach. They emphasise the fact that Iron Age coins turn up in great numbers in ritual deposits all over Europe, and from that observation conclude that coins were likely something quite different from money. Of course, even in our modern world, in which we often contrast our supposed rationality with the superstitions of earlier societies, coins are much more than just an exchange medium and a materialisation of value. The proliferation of coins that people toss into foundations, even in modern shopping malls, makes clear that some people think of coins as much more than money.

But Iron Age coins were something more than either money or material used for ritual offerings. Coins were the first mass-produced image-bearing objects in Europe. While fibulae and rings that bore figural imagery were all handcrafted individually, coins were mass-produced. We do not yet have the kind of settlement evidence that might allow us to say what proportion of people possessed coins, but the vast numbers of them minted suggests that they were widely distributed in the social system.

97

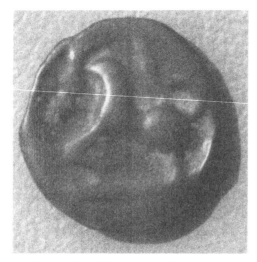

5.5. Bronze coin from
Late Iron Age Kelheim in
Bavaria, Germany;
diameter 1.8cm.

With a pair of dies and a hammer, coins with images on both sides could be minted at the rate of one every few seconds. Thus the 'value' of these image-bearing media would have been much lower than that of the jewellery with images on it and, in theory at least, many more people should have been able to have access to them. And there is no evidence to suggest that possession of them was restricted. At the oppidum settlement at Kelheim, for example, the four coins that we found in the course of excavations (Figure 5.5) all came from the cultural layer and were probably in the possession of people who lived in structures near where the coins were recovered.

Finds of coins and analyses of moulds for casting blanks and of dies makes apparent that many communities minted coins. All of the major *oppida* minted them, as did many smaller communities. The particular type of coin – the details of the design – was characteristic of a specific community. People thus shared the images on their coins with all of their fellow community members, as we do today, but our current community is a country that mints coins officially designed by those in charge of the government mint. Today we take hardly any notice of the

98

images on our coins, because we are so inundated with images. But when a new coin design is introduced, people take note and often set aside the first few of the new type that they receive, until they become common and thus no longer of interest.

In the US, the federal mint is issuing quarters (25-cent pieces) to commemorate the dates that the different states joined the union, with five issued each year. The new quarters all bear the same image on the obverse – George Washington in profile, surrounded by several texts. But the reverse commemorates the particular state in question. Each state must decide what image or combination of images it wants on 'its' quarter, and the debates about this indicate just how important these image-bearing media are even in our own time. The images on Iron Age coins must have been very important to the people who had them, especially when coinage was a novelty.

6

Images for magic and religion

In many societies, objects fashioned by craft workers, especially specialists such as blacksmiths and bronze workers, are believed to be imbued with some degree of magical power, as recent studies by Richard Hingley and Sandra Blakely show. Stephen Wilson's survey of magical beliefs associated with material culture in Europe's historical past provides some idea of the kinds of special powers that people in Iron Age and early medieval Europe are likely to have attributed to many of the objects they encountered in their daily lives. Regarding images in particular, W.J.T. Mitchell has written extensively on the magical associations that many people, including us, attribute to them. All the objects that I have been discussing in this book could reasonably be considered in a chapter on magic. But in this chapter, my focus is specifically on categories of material culture that appear to have had a primarily ritual purpose.

Defining the terms 'magic' and 'religion' is notoriously difficult. The subjects of this chapter are objects that early Europeans used in order to gain some control over their fates, to effect outcomes through application of images in particular ways.

Amulets

In their extensive study of amulets – objects believed to protect the bearer from misfortune – Liselotte Hansemann and Lenz Kriss-Rettenbeck show that natural items that are visually striking for some reason, and crafted images, most frequently serve this purpose. Most of the objects they discuss from both ancient and modern contexts share aspects of visual enhancement outlined earlier in Chapter 3. Many are images of humans and of animals, especially faces. Ludwig Pauli applied many of the principles outlined by those investigators to study amulets in prehistoric and early medieval Europe. While it is not possible to specify in the case of each individual object whether it was used as an amulet or not (and an object might serve as an amulet sometimes and not at others), Pauli showed that frequently the context in which such objects are found can provide information about how individual objects were used.

His study focuses largely on small figurines and animal-figure fibulae from graves at the Early Iron Age site of Hallstatt and at the later site at the Dürrnberg, both in Austria, but similar objects occur all over Europe. A woman's grave at Gündlingen in the upper Rhine valley dating to about 400 BC is an important recent discovery. Next to the lower part of her left leg was a deposit of objects, probably originally in a bag, of kinds often associated with amuletic or magical properties. Among them was a small figurine of a bull. One of the two bracelets she wore had on it two stylised human faces. A gold chain crafted about 800 years later with numerous small objects attached to it (we would call them 'charms' today) was found at Simleul Silvaniei in western Romania. Among the objects are a little canoe with a man in it, sheet gold leaves and numerous miniature tools and weapons. Attached is a crystal ball held by four bands of gold, with two tiny figures of lions. The size of the chain suggests that it was intended to be worn around the waist. In the case of some of the gold bracteates of the period AD 400-700, we are even better informed. These are circular discs with loops for suspension that were made in northern Europe and circulated widely over the continent. Well over 1,000 have been documented, and they turn up regularly on archaeological sites. While the great majority of the bracteates bear images of

6.1. Six gold bracteates from sites in Sweden.

animals and of humans (Figure 6.1), some include runic inscriptions as well, with texts such as 'I bring luck', that indicate the object's function as a charm.

Ritual places

During the Early Iron Age, communities in most parts of Europe practised tumulus burial for many of their members, thereby creating highly visible monuments to the rituals associated with the funerary ceremonies. During the fourth century BC, the practice of burial in tumuli declined (but did not disappear) from fashion, and flat grave cemeteries characterise the dominant material manifestations of funerary ritual thereafter. Around the time of this shift from mound burial to flat graves, communities in different parts of Europe began the practice of carrying out often large-scale rituals at open-air sites – places in which visibility for a substantial number of people seems to have been a major consideration. These places of ritual display were linked with three different media, each of which provided a distinctive surface on which the visual action took place. These media were earth (objects were displayed on the surface of the ground and deposited in pits and trenches); fire (offerings were placed in large fires, to be consumed or at least affected by the flames); and water (offerings were deposited into bodies of water).

Displays: earth

Open-air sanctuary sites at which large quantities of objects were displayed publicly for visual consumption and ultimately deposited in ditches and pits in the ground have been especially well documented in northern France. In the northeast of the country, Acy-Romance, Gournay-sur-Aronde and Ribemont have received particular attention. At Acy-Romance, excavations revealed a row of at least five sturdily built rectangular and oval structures, designated 'temples' by the excavators, all facing a large semicircular open space in which significant quantities of animal bones were recovered. Just northeast of the temple alignment were a series of unusual inhumation burials, with graves of men in contorted positions. Gournay-sur-Aronde and Ribemont show development of the practices evident earlier at Acy. Both sites included sturdily built enclosures, represented by postholes and foundation trenches, both contained in their interiors solid buildings that were not domestic in function, and both had postholes to support what are believed to have been displays of trophies – offensive and defensive weapons of different kinds acquired through victory in warfare. Life-size sculpted stone figures of humans have been identified at some of the sites, and it is highly likely that such figures were much more abundant than the relatively few finds suggest.

Displays: fire

Comparable in scale and in visual spectacle to the ritual sites of northern France, and to the weapon deposit sites in northern Europe (below), are the *Brandopferplätze* ('burned offering sites') of the hilly lands of the circum-Alpine region. Large quantities of tools and weapons, as well as personal ornaments and coins, were deposited at these sites in the course of rituals that involved large fires and slaughtering of animals. Werner Zanier's analysis of the recently excavated site at the Forggensee in southern Bavaria provides a good picture of one of these sites. In this case, the fire rituals were directly associated not only with the mountain landscape of the Bavarian Alps, but with water as well. The site shows ritual activity that included deposition of material between 100 BC and AD 250. Remains recovered included the bones of over 400 animals, of which 43 per cent were cattle and 57 per cent sheep and goat. The majority of the manufactured goods deposited at the site were of iron.

Displays: water

In terms of surfaces and textures, water provides unusual possibilities. As a surface, water can be smooth with no visible texture, as in a still woodland pond. In that state, it is a highly reflective surface, mirroring everything around it – trees, clouds, sky and animals or people who happen to be on the opposite bank. Under breezy conditions, and if the water is flowing as a river or stream, the surface changes from smooth to highly textured, and it loses its mirroring properties. Unlike the surface of the ground, the surface of water can be broken by tossing or dropping an object onto (into) it. That action causes a highly visible disturbance of the surface – a splash and, if the water is calm, outward-growing concentric circles. It also causes the object to disappear from the visible world. This act of removing objects from the visible world is analogous to the removal of objects from the sight of participants in funerary ceremonies when they are wrapped in textiles or placed into boxes during the ritual performance.

People have been making offerings in bodies of water since at least Neolithic times, and vast quantities of goods dating from the Bronze Age through the Middle Ages have been recovered in many places all over Europe. Such practices are still maintained today in many places, as at holy wells in Ireland and in fountains all over the world.

Images played an important role at such water deposit sites in early Europe. At Oberdorla in Thuringia, on the shores of a pond roughly 200 metres long by 70 metres wide (its size and shape changed over time), a ritual place was established at which ceremonies were performed over the course of a millennium, from around 500 BC to the second half of the first millennium AD. Most intensive use of the site was between about 200 BC and AD 300. In contrast to the places mentioned above, no weapons have been found at Oberdorla, but a wide range of other materials have been recovered. Most important for our purposes were anthropomorphic figurines carved of wood that had been set up in the soft ground as the visual foci for the rituals. More than 30 such figures have been identified. Many of the figurines are in the form of forked branches, where the two tines of the fork represent the two legs, and at the far end is a roughly sculpted neck and head. Other figures are more thoroughly formed, with recognisable eyes, nose and mouth. Other visually significant features of the site include animal skulls mounted on posts. Among other objects recovered through excavation and interpreted as offerings are bones of animals (both domestic and wild) and of humans, pottery, wooden vessels, tools and personal ornaments.

Carved wooden human effigies have been found in many

other places where favourable conditions of preservation have permitted the survival of wood. They indicate active use of wetlands in northern Europe during the pre-Roman Iron Age for ritual purposes. Characteristic are simple, stylised figures, most often of oak. Torsten Capelle notes that such objects do not occur in graves and therefore seem to be public images, meant to be seen by many people.

Flemming Kaul (2003: 34) provides a vivid reconstruction of how the visual aspect of such wooden figurines might have been used in ritual, specifically in relation to the 2.74 metre tall oak figure from Forlev Nymølle in Jutland:

> The tall wooden idol, perhaps painted or in colourful robes, is carried forward at the head of the procession, and finally raised up a little out in the lake. In the procession walk the inhabitants of the area, and several of them are carrying a set of long, new and almost white ash poles, which are perhaps knocked or banged against one another to make a noise. In the end they too are placed in the lake, and depending on the event the offering begins with the placing of earthenware vessels with contents, broken wooden objects, parts of animals, charcoal heaps, bunches of flax and, as a central element, the dumping and throwing of white stones. By virtue of their length both the idol and the staves could be easily seen, and they may have been markers at which one threw the white stones with the object of 'drowning' these wooden objects, and people would have thrown until they lay anchored to the lake bottom.

About 30 major weapon deposits have been identified in bogs in northern Europe, of which those at Hjortspring, Vimose, Nydam, Thorsberg and Illerup are particularly well documented examples. Characteristic of these sites are hundreds of

6. Images for magic and religion

6.2. Bronze face from the weapon deposit at Vimose, Denmark; height 3.3cm.

weapons, including swords, lances, spears, shields and helmets. At the site of Illerup, for example, during the years between AD 200 and 500, people deposited, on successive occasions, a great quantity of objects in a body of water measuring about 200 by 400 metres. The objects recovered by archaeologists include 225 swords, 660 spearheads, 745 lance points, remains of at least 430 shields, together with arrowheads, axes and metal attachments associated with harness gear for horses. In some cases the bodies of water in which the weapons were deposited have become bogs; in others they remain open water. Analysis of the patterns of deposition of the hundreds and even thousands of objects shows that the rituals during which the objects were deposited into the water were highly visual affairs. The objects deposited included a wide range of complex images, many of animals and some of humans (Figure 6.2).

Weapons and other equipment were often purposely destroyed by smashing them with axes and other implements before being deposited. These actions must have been both visually and aurally powerful – the sight and sound of precious metal weapons and vessels being pounded, dented and flattened in the course of the ritual. Witnessing the act of depositing, whether by heaving objects from the shore or dropping them from boats, was also visually memorable. Serviceable, valuable and often strikingly beautiful objects were dramatically removed from the visible world to disappear forever beneath the surface of the water.

Vessels for ritual

From the Late Bronze Age (1200-800 BC) onwards, metal vessels played important roles in ritual. They often bear complex iconographic elements, and they are frequently recovered in deposits that are interpreted as offerings. From the earliest textual sources for northern Europe, we have references to the special roles that such vessels played in myth and legend.

The Gundestrup cauldron from northern Jutland, and the pair of gold horns from Gallehus in southern Denmark, are covered with pictorial imagery. Although many scholars have attempted to explain the meaning of the figures on the vessels, none have been able to offer explanations that have convinced the scholarly world. The principal problem is that, as noted earlier (see Chapter 1), while the imagery on these vessels may relate to specific stories or religious beliefs, those changed over time, while materialisations of them, such as the scenes on these metal vessels, do not.

The Gundestrup cauldron is similar in some respects to many bronze cauldrons, but it is unique in being of silver, with gilding on many of the figures on the exterior plates and glass eyes inset into some of the faces originally. With a mouth diameter of 69cm, the Gundestrup cauldron is larger than most of the bronze cauldrons. Its size, colour and texture make it a visually stunning piece, even seen from a distance, and from close up, the prevalence of faces and the high relief ornament hold the viewer's attention. The object was found in a bog in 1891 without any other items, hence it is difficult to associate it with any particular behaviour, such as feasting. Everything about it suggests that it was meant to be displayed and seen, and to be examined up close as well as viewed from a distance. Only from up close could a viewer see the complex interior panels. We do not know whether every member of the community was initiated into the meaning of the representations, or whether that kind of significance was shared by only an elite few. On the basis of stylistic study the Gundestrup cauldron is thought to have been made around 100 BC, although a later date is also possible. (Much debate revolves around where it was made, but there is no reason why it could not have been made in Denmark.)

The Gallehus horns, which are not an exact pair, were found at the same location, one in 1639, the other in 1734. Based on the techniques used in manufacturing them, on some of the motifs used, and on the character of the runes on one, they are believed to have been made around AD 400 in southern Scandinavia. As with the Gundestrup cauldron, many different explanations have been offered for the complex iconography of the figures on the horns, but none is fully satisfying. While the figures represented on the Gundestrup cauldron are in relief, pressed out from the back, with subsequent detailing to refine the images, the figures on the Gallehus horns are in some cases cast and attached as appliqués, in other cases outlined with dots.

Like the cauldron, the horns are of a form common in well outfitted burials, such as those at Hochdorf and Sutton Hoo. They are unique in being substantially of gold, and they are large (but not as large as the iron drinking horn at Hochdorf), the complete one being 75.8cm long (the other was probably the same length originally). Since drinking horns played special roles in ritual associated with elites in political and religious contexts, the horns were important visual objects. And the numerous and varied figures and symbols on the horns would have captivated viewers who were able to get close enough to examine the details.

Ornate metal vessels designed to be used in Christian religious services provide another set of important visual objects associated with ritual performance. The Ardagh Chalice was made in the early eighth century, the Tassilo Chalice in the latter part of that century. It is important to note that they are part of a tradition going back at least to the ornate bronze jugs of Basse-Yutz and the Glauberg, with visually striking figural ornament used as a means of attracting and holding viewers' attention for particular purposes.

As Christian chalices, both vessels were intended to be the visual focus of the most important ritual in the Christian Church, the mass. Like many of the attention-getting objects we have examined already, these vessels use texture, colour and glitter to focus the attention of participants. The shape of both objects is clear from a distance. But both have on their surfaces intricately fine relief ornament that can only be seen close up, as was the case with the Chessel Down and Donzdorf fibulae and the Sutton Hoo buckle. They invite viewers to approach, to get a closer look, if they are permitted to do so.

The body of the Ardagh Chalice, 15cm high, is silver. The bowl is separated from the foot by a highly textured and ornate gold column (Figure 6.3). The top of the vessel is bounded by a distinct rim, as is the outer edge of the foot. From a distance, most of the surface of the chalice seems to be smooth silver, with a pair of vertical handles on the sides and with a relief band of gold ornament around the upper part of the body, with colourful studs at intervals, and with raised silver ridges bounding the gold band above and below. On two sides are circular ornaments, with delicate gold filigree and with five coloured knobs, with red and blue enamel and glass. The handles have on them gold filigree and cells of red and green enamel, and just below each handle is another attachment with includes zones of gold filigree and knobs of red and green enamel. While the basic shape is apparent from a considerable distance away, the detailed shapes of the gold interweave, the filigree and the exquisitely divided knobs can only be discerned from a few feet away. It is only when the viewer approaches very close – a foot or so away – that he or she sees that just below the gold band the silver is covered with tiny dots, and in the pattern of dots

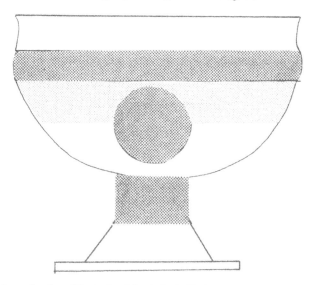

6.3. Schematic plan of the body of the Ardagh Chalice (without the handles), indicating portions bearing complex textured ornament that is visible at a distance (dark shading) and the much more subtle pattern of fine dots and names of the apostles that can only be seen at very close range (light shading).

are the names of the apostles. And of course to read these names, the viewer not only needs to be very close to the object – a privilege perhaps reserved for just a few – but also has to be literate, a state still limited in eighth-century Ireland. The object has all of the elements of visual complexity discussed earlier in Chapter 3.

The Tassilo Chalice is different, but no less visually captivating. It stands 27cm high. Like the Ardagh Chalice, it is divided into three main parts, the bowl at the top, a joining neck and the foot. The Tassilo Chalice is made of hammered copper, silver plated, and with gold coating on the entire inside surface and on parts of the outside. Unlike the Ardagh Chalice, with its extensive portions of the exterior consisting of smooth silver, the entire exterior surface of the Tassilo Chalice is covered with decoration. All is divided into zones of different shapes. Some contain images of humans, others intricate interlace ornament. Like the Ardagh Chalice, it too also bears an inscription, informing the literate viewer about who commissioned the piece.

Cologne woman's grave

In the course of construction work in 1959 under the floor of the choir of the Cologne Cathedral, the grave of a woman was found in a small chapel, the foundation of which lay beneath the cathedral. This location associates the grave with early Christianity in the region. The woman was buried around AD 525, in a wooden coffin that had been placed into a stone sarcophagus. She was interred with abundant personal ornaments, including earrings, a bracelet, two finger rings, four fibulae, two gold chains, necklaces of glass and amber beads and Roman coins and ornaments on her shoes. Most of these objects were made of gold, and many were inlaid with garnet. At her waist she wore a belt, fastened with an ornate buckle, with tools attached to it, including shears, a knife, a pendant and a bulla.

Like the Hochdorf and Sutton Hoo graves, she was buried with a substantial set of feasting vessels. But in contrast to those other two graves, here there were no two vessels that were alike. The implication is that the vessels were all for her use, and did not reflect her serving a party of others. Six vessels were of glass, two were of bronze, and one was a horn shaped into a drinking vessel. There was also a wooden box at the opposite end of the sarcophagus from the woman's head, and in it were slippers, gold braid, nuts and seeds, a rock crystal bead and a clay spindle whorl. Remains of textiles show that in this grave too, they played an important role. A woollen blanket had been placed over the woman at the final stage of arranging the grave.

This grave is of special interest to our consideration of visual expression of religion and ritual, because on the one hand, it has significant Christian elements, and on the other, it has important traditional, non-Christian ones. The clearest non-Christian aspects include the practice of burial with lavish goods, including a feasting set, and numerous animal ornaments characteristic of local practices. But the location within a chapel, the forerunner to the later churches on the site, is a Christian aspect. Furthermore there are at least three crosses represented among the objects in the burial. One is on the bulla, another on the upper end of the knife handle and the third on one of the pair of bow fibulae.

The pair of bow fibulae are of special interest, as the results of a study by Claus von Carnap-Bornheim indicate. The two are made of gold with garnet inlay, with complex patterns of filigree along the bows. They are 7.5cm long, the large flat head plates measure 3.6 by 2.2cm. The two head plates are similar, each comprised of 26 cells topped with cut garnet and with waffled gold foil under the garnet pieces, giving the objects very bright, glittering character. The feet of the two fibulae are slightly different. One has a cross in a roundel just before the end of the foot, while the other is divided by a three-armed shape into four cells.

Carnap-Bornheim's study raises important questions about the visual impact of these fibulae. Here we have a fine example of visual reception depending on local knowledge, or, in this case, on close familiarity with artistic conventions of this period. To the inexperienced eye, the head plate would probably look like a design formed by the break-up of the surface by the cell edges. But if you know what to look for in representations in this period, you may note that in the middle of the head is a circle of garnet that forms the eye for two beaks of birds of prey, one facing left and one facing right. Once that image is pointed out, it is impossible to look at the fibulae without immediately seeing it. But there is much more to the pattern than just the double bird head. The circle can also be seen to form the body of an insect, with wings on either side. In the other cells, Carnap-Bornheim identifies facing griffons and a predatory animal. Once these have been pointed out, they seem obvious. But most us would never notice them on our own. In seeing them, we can appreciate why the head plate of these fibulae is shaped so unusually.

What was the intention of this complex and 'hidden' set of images? Did the images remain secret to most people who saw the fibulae, and were they intended to provide some kind of secret power or influence to the owner? Or, as Leslie Webster has suggested for some comparable complex objects in the Anglo-Saxon world, could these bear images that were meant to be seen and understood by a small group of cognoscenti, leaving the majority of people in the society in the dark? And what is the connection between these puzzling fibula images and the Christian location and crosses? Are these disparate signs that happened to come together in this grave, or is there a reason why these fibulae are in a context associated with signs of the new religion?

Illuminated manuscripts

The illuminated manuscript was a new medium of visual expression for religious themes that achieved a spectacular level of development in the British Isles during the seventh and eighth centuries. The Lindisfarne Gospels, created about 695, will serve as an example here. Like all the other objects of visual display discussed in this chapter, the purpose of the dazzling images was to attract and hold the attention of members of the social community to which Christian officials were ministering.

Especially interesting is the fact that the decorative patterns, animal motifs and even design details in the Lindisfarne Gospels employ the same techniques that we have seen in the metalwork from the prehistoric Iron Age through the early medieval period, as Janet Backhouse's analysis has shown. The curvilinear forms, trumpet shapes and peltas are all very similar to those on metal ornaments and vessels, and the artist has used techniques to make the shapes in the book appear to be three-dimensional. Interlace patterns, similar to those on the Sutton Hoo buckle, are represented in extreme detail on the 'carpet pages', together with animals, including dogs and birds, that look very like their three-dimensional metal counterparts. Some pages have thousands of tiny dots of red paint creating textured surfaces, very similar to the way that niello points add texture to many metal ornaments and tiny impressed dots created texture for parts of the Ardagh Chalice that were otherwise unadorned.

7

Images in landscapes

As we consider the visuality of the landscapes of early Europe, we must bear in mind that to a greater extent than for the categories of evidence discussed in Chapters 4, 5 and 6, the material evidence pertaining to the visual quality of landscapes has been most severely damaged since the cultural landscapes of early Europe were created. Objects such as the Donzdorf fibulae survive essentially as they were created, undisturbed burials such as Hochdorf and Cologne Cathedral provide us with complete assemblages of objects in their original arrangements, and even ritual sites such as Gournay, Oberdorla and Illerup allow us to study original patterns of deposition, since they were buried and thus largely protected from modern disturbance. But no landscape in Europe survives as it looked two millennia ago. Huge numbers of sites of visual importance have been destroyed by agriculture and construction. In open land, burial mounds have been ploughed flat, and standing stone structures knocked down and broken up for building material.

Landscapes as surfaces

By the start of the Early Iron Age, the landscape of temperate Europe was already marked with countless monuments of the past. Megalithic tombs, standing stones, stone circles, burial mounds, hill fort walls, banks and ditches from many different periods of the past covered most landscapes to a greater or lesser degree. In their midst were the structures of the early

European present, the houses, outbuildings, fences, banks and ditches, fields and their boundaries, and other aspects of the cultural landscape.

To adopt Gibson's concepts, all landscapes are surfaces, with textures and affordances. In contrast to the places considered earlier in Chapter 5, and some of those in Chapter 6, landscapes are out-of-doors and as such are ordinarily much better illuminated than interior or sheltered spaces. Light comes from the sun above and is diffused in all directions as it hits the ground, foliage, rocks and structures built on the surface. Under ordinary daytime conditions, seeing is aided in the landscape by the profusion of light. Because natural light changes constantly – with the time of day, the season, the weather, the passing clouds – the visuality of the landscape is an ever-changing phenomenon.

In contrast to the spaces considered in Chapters 5 and 6, that in landscapes is unlimited. Unless something blocks the view, the observer can see as far as the horizon. Any structures created by humans – burial mounds or carved stones, for example – break the view to the horizon, and become figures in front of the background. Burial chambers are sealed, and objects disappear from sight. At sites of water deposits, the objects disappear from sight as they fall through the surface of the water. But in cultural landscapes, objects remain visible day after day.

The texture of the surface of the land varies greatly, and that texture affects its visuality. Flat grassland or meadow, such as in the Hungarian Plain or parts of Denmark, provides a clear line of sight for miles. Structures erected by people, such as megalithic tombs and Bronze Age burial mounds, stand out sharply against the horizon. Hilly and rocky lands, such as the foothills of the Vosges Mountains or of the Carpathians, create rougher and much more uneven textures, in which standing objects can be more difficult to discern. In forests, visability is much more limited.

Any visual break, or disruption, in the surface of the landscape is significant for people and for animals. Interruptions of the landscape surface have long served as places of ritual activity. All over Europe since at least Neolithic times, people have made deposits in springs and ponds, next to cliffs and rock outcroppings and in caves and fissures. At least from the time that the first farmers of Europe began clearing forest to open lands for cultivation, and some communities began constructing megalithic monuments, people have been creating cultural landscapes. In the Early Iron Age, fields of tumuli were powerful visual agents in shaping people's ideas about the landscapes they inhabited and about their relations with the natural world in (and beyond) those landscapes.

Landscapes as backgrounds

In many different kinds of visual studies, ranging from archaeological surveys or analyses of monuments to painters' creations of portraits or town scenes, landscape plays the passive role of background, in a sense similar to Gombrich's treatment of the concept of background discussed above (see Chapter 2). Things happen in landscapes, but rarely are landscapes seen as active agents in human affairs. But landscapes afford many of the visual enhancements discussed earlier in Chapter 3. Landscapes include surfaces, they are textured, they can be complex, depending on what combinations of natural (trees, bushes, rocks) or cultural (houses, fences) elements are present. And landscapes afford the lighting for everything that happens in them. Lighting is a particularly important aspect of landscapes, because it changes constantly and dramatically. Clouds darken the sun's rays. When the moon is bright, it can illuminate much in a landscape. As Mitchell observes, the landscape has a special role in providing the setting for the interaction of humans with the natural world.

118

7. *Images in landscapes*

Landscape and memory

Landscapes provide powerful connections to memory, both for individuals and for groups. Human actions of the past are directly visible in the landscape. Past ceremonies, celebrations, battles and funerary rituals can be directly recalled through viewing of the standing stones, banks and ditches, and mounds that were created for such occasions. In this general sense, any landscape tells the story of its past, geological, biological and human. More specifically for early Europe, burial mounds remind us of ancestors, megalithic tombs of more distant progenitors, perhaps mythical rather than historical. In many instances, the structures within cultural landscapes are powerfully significant not only because of associations with the distant past, but also because current rituals are performed at them. In our own times, we see rituals performed at war memorials, and Stonehenge still attracts celebrants every summer. Historic sites of battles are significant landscapes for ceremonial celebration in the modern world.

John Barrett, Christopher Tilley and Tim Ingold have contributed to landscape studies by their emphasis of the need for the researcher to experience the landscape himself or herself in order to gain some sense of what it was like for the person at the time. This goal is difficult to achieve – some would say impossible – because the landscape of today is very different from that of 2,000 years ago. We can spend time in landscapes in which a substantial number of standing monuments are still visible on the surface, and we can also experience the landscapes of the present day, and use our experiences in them to think about what the ancient landscapes were like for Europeans of the past.

Of all of the possible structures in the visible landscape that I might have included here, I have selected sculptured stones of the Iron Age, the Glauberg earthworks, halls, Irish High

Crosses and landscape carvings such as the Uffington White Horse for brief consideration.

Sculptured stones of the Iron Age

Numerous sculptured anthropomorphic stones of Iron Age date have been known for some time, such as those from Calw, Heidelberg, Holzgerlingen, Pfalzfeld and Waldenbuch in Germany, and from numerous sites in France. Others have been discovered more recently in the course of systematic excavations, notably at Hirschlanden, Vix and the Glauberg. Zürn's reconstruction of the position of the Hirschlanden statue places it on top of a burial mound, a situation similar to that of the similar-sized stone statues on some of the enormous mounds in eastern Europe, in the region associated with the peoples known as Scythians. At Vix, the life-size sculptures of a seated woman and man are associated with what seems to have been an enclosure in which feasting rituals were carried out in conjunction with the arrangement of the rich woman's burial nearby. At the Glauberg, the magnificently well-preserved statue is just one of four, the other three very fragmentary, found next to the tumulus that contained two well outfitted graves. The excavators think that the four statues were set up close to the tumulus, just northwest of its perimeter.

These recent discoveries suggest that statues were relatively abundant in Iron Age Europe. Places where many tumuli were situated, and especially the large tumuli that often contained richly outfitted Early Iron Age graves, such as those at Mont Lassois, the Heuneburg and the Hohenasperg, probably had many of these figures standing on or next to the mounds. Today in some landscapes we can appreciate the extraordinary visual power of fields of tumuli, but of course most have been ploughed away and all have been eroded to heights much less than their originals. But with many of the stone statues standing on or

7. Images in landscapes

7.1. Reconstructed Early Iron Age burial mound at Kilchberg in southwestern Germany, with stylised anthropomorphic stele on top.

near the tumuli, the landscape of these Iron Age cemeteries must have been striking visual spectacles (Figure 7.1).

The statues were ordinarily made from local sandstone, and today they are often coarsely textured in appearance. Some, if not all, were probably originally painted in bright colours, as recent study of the well-known figure from Roquepertuse in southern France has shown that that figure was. The nearly complete statues all show visually significant material insignia – conical hat, neck ring, dagger and belt for Hirschlanden; neck ring for the woman at Vix; and sword, shield, neck ring, bracelet and finger ring for Glauberg. Even though they were better protected covered by soil than they would have been exposed to the weather, all of the statues are in weathered condition – they must have looked quite different when they were new.

Investigators have noted that in many traditional societies, landscape features are associated with ancestors or with spirits of various kinds. Folktales recorded in the nineteenth century tell of supernatural visions experienced by individuals travelling about the countryside at night. One set of stories tells of people walking past burial mounds and hearing sounds of fairies partying inside, surely a modern interpretation of beliefs about the spiritual power of these monuments in the landscape.

As a careful look at the stones will indicate, these were very striking objects. And we need to take account of the fact that today we see them mounted in museum displays, not in the environments in which they were erected originally. Standing atop mounds or arranged near mounds, they created powerful visions through their shape, size, colour and texture. As Tilley has observed about standing stones, they seem to change with the changing directions of the sunlight, with clear or cloudy conditions, with mist or rain or snow. Some of the statues were sculpted to look relatively realistic, such as Hirschlanden, Vix and Glauberg, whereas others were highly stylised (Figure 7.1). These monuments probably looked partly as if they were human and partly as if they were part of the natural landscape, since all of the stones used were coarse and textured, none smooth or polished, as Classical Greek statues were.

Glauberg earthworks

Research at the Glauberg has revealed an extensive and complex series of earthworks associated with the tumulus and the statue there. Perhaps similar earthworks accompanied many burials in Iron Age Europe, and it is only a special set of circumstances that brought these to light at the Glauberg. The site presented a striking visual spectacle to accompany the funerary ceremony around 400 BC and to remind people of that ritual and its meaning for a long time thereafter.

The mound at the Glauberg was sizeable but not unusually large by Early Iron Age standards. Its diameter was 48 metres, and its height is estimated to have been about 6 metres. It was part of an elaborate system of ditches that extended far into the landscape. Around the mound was a circular ditch about 10 metres wide and over 3 metres deep. At the southeastern part of the circular ditch, rather than closing to form a complete circle, the two parts of the ditch connect to two parallel ditches that continue in a straight line toward the southwest, lining an open passage about 10 metres wide. The ditches are each about 7 metres wide and 3 metres deep, and they extend for 350 metres. At the end, the western ditch turns sharply and extends on to the west, the eastern ditch turns and extends to the east.

The setting of the funeral of one or both of the individuals who were buried in the tumulus must have been an impressive affair. The great ditches formed an avenue – a broad strip of land 350 metres long and 10 metres wide that led in a straight line toward the tumulus. Next to the tumulus stood the four life-size statues of men. In the background loomed the hilltop settlement on the Glauberg, with massive walls against the sky. If we consider this complex in relation to the texture of surface, we are looking at a series of visually striking and complex objects. The ditches represent a disturbance in the texture of the ground surface by penetrating into the earth, while the avenue is a part of the surface apparently left untouched. At the end of the avenue, centred on its axis, is the mound, and next to it the stone statues, all situated beneath the hill fort.

How common the situation at the Glauberg was, with the extensive ditch system around it, is not clear at the present time. Recent investigations around the Heuneburg suggest that such a complex of earthworks may not have been unusual at Early Iron Age centres.

Halls

Historically, halls were the places where Roman emperors and other officials held their formal audiences, and where early medieval kings practised similar activities, as portrayed in *Beowulf* and elsewhere. Archaeologically unusually large and spacious buildings appear in northern Europe beginning around the third century with Gudme on Fyn in Denmark and Uppåkra in southern Sweden. In Anglo-Saxon England, we know of such structures at Yeavering in Northumbria, and at other sites. Charlemagne's complex of chapel and hall constructed at Aachen at the end of the eighth century marries the traditions of the Roman audience hall with the northern European king's hall and with the structures of early Christianity.

When these halls are explored archaeologically, they typically yield objects that make their special political and ritual roles clear. At Gudme and Uppåkra, large quantities of gold, imported luxuries and extraordinary local crafts and representational objects, including figurines, have been recovered. Since the architecture was of wood, little survives of the exterior structure of these buildings. But based on sources that describe the early halls as richly ornate, and on what we know of later buildings of similar purpose in northern Europe, specialists reconstruct these halls with lavish animal ornament on the outside. In their reconstruction of the recently excavated hall at Uppåkra, for example, Larsson and Lenntorf envisage exterior roof beams with carved serpent heads at the ends, and elaborately carved corner post timbers with intricate animal ornament, similar to that on metalwork of the period.

High Crosses of Ireland

The Irish High Crosses were parts of a much broader pattern of stone crosses in the northern regions of the British Isles (Figure 7.2). Some investigators argue that there was no previous tradition in Ireland of architecture in stone, and that the High Crosses thus represent something new. But from the point of the visuality, and of visually important interruptions in the surface of the landscape, the High Crosses played roles similar to those of the abundant megalithic monuments of Neolithic

7.2. High Cross at Kells, Ireland, known as the 'Cross of Saints Patrick and Columba'. Height 3.3m.

and Bronze Age times, and of the ogham stones. In this sense, the High Crosses represent a continuation of a tradition of standing stones from the Neolithic Period on. Ogham stones are thought to have been erected during the fifth, sixth and seventh centuries, and thus can be considered immediate predecessors to the High Crosses. Ogham stones are stones set upright in the ground with markings in the ogham script along one edge. The script consists of groups of lines incised into the stone, on either side of a corner and across the corner. They were for the most part memorials to deceased individuals. They occur most abundantly in the south of Ireland, but are also found in all other parts of Ireland, in southern Wales, and scattered in other parts of the British Isles, especially in Cornwall and in northeastern Scotland.

The Irish High Crosses are believed to have first been sculpted and erected in the middle of the seventh century, and to have continued to be created into the twelfth. Around 300 still survive today, ranging from fairly simply decorated, to those ornamented with pattern motifs, to those with scenes from the Bible and of the crucifixion. They can stand as high as 6 metres and are thus very imposing monuments. The design patterns and pictorial themes connect with ornamented metalwork of the period on the one hand, and with manuscript illumination on the other. A large proportion, if not all, of the High Crosses were erected at or near monasteries.

Visually, the High Crosses played a role similar to that of the megalithic monuments (tombs, standing stones, circles) of the earlier periods, and of the sculpted stones of Iron Age continental Europe. They were pieces of local stone, sculpted into a form specific to their cultural context, set firmly in the ground, and intended to communicate visually with people who saw them. All of these structures were relatively tall and thin, and all created interruptions in the line of the horizon, like many other stone monuments of early Europe, including Roman tombstones, Jupiter-Giant columns of the Rhine and Danube provinces of the Roman Empire, and the picture stones of early medieval Gotland.

Uffington White Horse

The Uffington White Horse is something very different. It is also an interruption in the surface of the landscape, but in this case, it is an interruption in an interruption. It is an enormous figure of a horse, around 110 metres long, carved into the chalk

7.3. Drawing of the Uffington White Horse in Oxfordshire, UK, showing
members of the local community in the middle of the nineteenth century
working to maintain its form by clearing away vegetation and debris.

hillside overlooking a valley in south-central England. It is one
of a number of figures of animals and anthropomorphic figures cut
into the sides of hills. The dating of the figure has been the subject
of much debate over the years. Topographically, it is closely
associated with an Iron Age hill fort, but the carved figure is
difficult to date using any of the common techniques of dating late
prehistoric or early historic monuments. Recent studies conducted
by Gosden and Lock suggest that the figure was probably originally carved into the chalk surface sometime during the Late
Bronze or Early Iron Age. Significantly, in order for the figure to
remain visible, vegetation and soil need to be cleared away regularly, and the cleaning of the White Horse seems to have been a
local traditional practice for a very long time (Figure 7.3).

Its uniqueness and its scale distinguish the Uffington White Horse from all of the other categories of landscape visual features discussed here. Although there are other early figures carved into the chalk, this is the only horse carved in this particular style, similar to the style used in horse representations on many different categories of Iron Age coins. While the various kinds of standing stones discussed above break the continuity of the surface with a single vertical shaft, this figure instead communicates visually by its situation on a natural feature that interrupts the surface of the ground. Its appearance signals to the viewer the special character of the place where it is situated.

The need for regular clearing of the figure is an indication of the importance of this visual monument to the people who created it and to many generations of people who have lived in the area since then. The fact that it has not disappeared under the vegetation over the millennia attests to the regular interest and efforts of people to keep it cleared – to maintain is visibility.

8

Images and visuality

My approach in this book has been to examine images as visual objects, rather than to interpret them as 'meaning' something else, with regard to what we commonly call religion, or myth or political consciousness. As I have tried to show, by approaching images from the perspective of their visuality, and paying close attention to the contexts – in the broadest sense – in which the objects are recovered, we can begin to develop an appreciation for how the visual qualities of things were used to elicit responses in people. The placement of visually complex objects on certain places on the body of the deceased, the arrangement of feasting vessels in a tomb chamber, the position of images on a site at which ritual deposits were made and the way that stone stele were set into the landscape can all provide us with information about how these crafted things were used and how people responded to them.

Status and imagery

The great majority of images, and always the most complex images, were associated with social elites. But these elite associations do not mean that the majority of people did not see images. As we have seen throughout this book, images were used to ornament visually distinctive objects, such as the Hochdorf neck ring, the Donzdorf fibulae and the Sutton Hoo buckle – all objects that were designed to be seen at a distance, by large numbers of people. At feasts hosted by individuals such as the man at Hochdorf and the king at Sutton Hoo, many people besides the elite would have attended and marvelled at the extraordinarily large and ornate vessels like the cauldrons, the drinking horns, the jugs and the dishes. Rituals carried out at Gournay-sur-Aronde, Oberdorla and Illerup included large numbers of participants, although the ceremonies were most likely conducted by elites. And certainly most people in and around places such as the Glauberg and the monastic sites where the High Crosses were erected became accustomed to seeing great sculpted stone monuments forming striking elements of their landscapes. Even though the visually complex objects were firmly in the hands of the elite, everyone in society participated in seeing and responding to them. An exploration of the visual worlds of members of the much larger non-elite groups during these times would surely repay the effort. Detailed study of objects from typical graves and settlements would surely produce meaningful results.

Vision and visual enhancement

Craft workers and visual enhancement

In Chapter 2, I reviewed some salient points regarding current understanding among neuroscientists and cognitive psychologists about how humans see. Of particular relevance for the materials examined in this book is the way the human brain selects subjects on which to focus, how the eyes scan surfaces and fix on certain features and how our cognitive map develops. The early Europeans who made and saw the images discussed in this book had cognitive maps different from ours, because their experience seeing and otherwise perceiving their environment was different. And as a result of seeing and responding to images such as those we have considered, they developed a different view of their world from the views we have of ours.

The craft workers who made the objects we have discussed

created those of 'visual complexity' with some understanding of how they could exploit the way that their contemporaries saw in order to achieve their aims of crafting images that attracted and held people's attention. These objects were surely perceived by many as magical, in that they enchanted viewers to fix their gaze on them, to move closer, to seek to understand all the complexities before them. On some level, a large proportion of crafted objects are regarded in traditional societies as magical, imbued with special powers. For images, this property is accentuated. Many images are thought to be alive, to be sentient beings, to possess spirits. Probably the majority of the objects discussed in this book, with their dazzling glitter and sometimes fantastically complex array of ambiguous decoration, held magical powers for the people who gazed at them.

Contexts of use and deposition

As cognitive psychologists demonstrate through experiment, what humans see depends very heavily on context. The greatest challenge we have in trying to understand how people 2,000 years ago saw the objects we study is that we can never reconstruct the context in which they saw them, whether that was in a burial, being tossed into a pond or standing on top of a burial mound. Even the issue of lighting is vital in trying to understand how objects were perceived visually, as I have suggested in the discussion above.

Why enhance visually?

The ultimate purpose of creating visually complex objects was social – for building, asserting, maintaining and expressing social relationships between individuals and groups. In Chapters 4-7 I suggested approaches to visually potent objects with respect to different kinds of social relationships. Of course the categories I use – individual, group, ritual and landscape – are artificial and probably would not have been recognised by the people whom we are studying, but it provides a means for organising the discussion. Put into simple terms, the visually potent objects linked to individuals – placed on their bodies in their graves, or arranged next to them – served to structure, in the minds of the participants in the funeral ceremony, their relationships with the deceased and with members of the deceased individual's family and social group. In the context of communal meals and feasts, the visually enhanced objects served to create stronger social bonds between the individuals participating, whether they were of equal status or of different status. The same point applies to coins, where every person who might possess a coin and the images on it was linked to every other person who possessed an object with the same image, but also linked to the individual or group that controlled the minting process – the supply of metal, the dies and the technology of minting. In ritual contexts, the role of the visually enhanced images was to connect all participants in the ritual in their social group, particularly in respect to their sharing of religious beliefs and experiences and their participation in the process of religious ritual.

Distance and detail

The design of so many objects in such a way that we can see some of the character of the piece from a distance, but more as we approach for a closer view, strongly suggests that it was the intention of the wearer that some visual information should be available to many, but other information should be restricted to people who were allowed to come close. I discussed this point using the Chessel Down fibula as an example (see Chapter 4), but the same principle applies to most of the visually complex objects of personal use – the Hochdorf neck ring, the Glauberg and Donzdorf fibulae and the Sutton Hoo buckle. This differentiation between what could be seen and understood at a distance, and what could be seen only at very close range, supports the theory that people of different status, and of different relationship to the wearer, had different levels of visual access to these objects. This principle also applies to the two Christian vessels considered and to the Lindisfarne Gospels. Like the complex fibulae, these images require very close scrutiny if one is to see all of the intricate detail. As with the personal ornaments, the question arises, were these ritual objects designed to present one visual aspect to one group of people, and another to a different group?

Coins present a different situation. With Iron Age coins, we saw the first instance of mass production of images, such that many people could possess and see closely the same images. Significantly, the coins bear only simple, not visually complex (according to the definition in Chapter 3) images. Evidence of coin distributions suggests that the widespread sharing of coins and the images they bore was a way that members of communities in the Late Iron Age felt some degree of belonging to a single group, at a time that many communities were growing much larger and more diverse than any earlier ones in temperate Europe.

Subtle visual distinctions

Some patterns in the display of images and decoration are puzzling to a modern mind, and their presence suggests that there are many visual indicators that remain hidden to us, until we find ways to discover them. Von Carnap-Bornheim's discernment of a whole series of animals 'hidden' in the ornament of the head ends of the two gold-and-garnet fibulae in the Cologne woman's grave is a good example of such patterns that have generally not been recognised by modern researchers. Another example is the subtle difference between the feet of

133

those two fibulae. One has a small cross in the gold-and-garnet pattern; the other does not. This difference is not immediately obvious to a viewer and would not be seen at a distance, but since the cross is an important sign of the new religion, this difference between the two objects may have been an important sign borne by this woman.

The bird heads represented on military equipment during the Roman Iron Age are another example of what seem to be subtle variations on visual themes (Chapter 3). In some instances, they are represented with long pointed beaks and blue glass eyes. In others, only the hint of a beak is present, and no eyes are indicated, but the shape of the head clearly refers to the theme 'bird of prey'. (The 'meaning' of the bird of prey sign is outside the scope of this book.)

From visibility to memory

In a number of elite graves that we have considered, there is good evidence that, as part of the funerary ceremony, objects that had played important visual roles in the proceedings were removed from the visual environment in the course of the ritual. Analysis of the textile remains at Hochdorf suggest that all of the objects in the grave were wrapped in fabrics before the chamber was sealed. At Sutton Hoo also, textiles seem to have played an important role in the covering of objects in the grave, and the man's prized personal ornaments were placed into a box that was set into the full grave arrangement. In the Cologne woman's grave, a number of important objects were set into a box. At the Glauberg, the two jugs were placed into textile wrappers, and at München-Perlach and other sites of its period, ornate fibulae were set into textile sheaths. Since textiles rarely are recovered in the course of excavations, it is likely that the use of fabrics in funerary rituals was much more widespread than present evidence indicates.

8. Images and visuality

The act of removing objects from the visual field of the participants in the funerary ceremonies, by placing them in boxes or in textile containers, or by wrapping them or covering them with textiles, was an important part of the visual display in these rituals. Observers who witnessed the process of covering significant objects would have formed powerful memories of the process, and these memories may have been much more potent than what they would have remembered if they had simply seen the burial chambers sealed and covered with earth. The wrapping of objects served to draw special attention to them, not wholly unlike the results of the artist Christo's wrapping of buildings and bridges in our time.

Continuities and variations of visual representation

Continuities

An important result to emerge from this study is the consistency of the way that visual images were used from the Early Iron Age through to the early medieval period. This consistency is apparent in the similarities in the display of individual ornaments in burials at Hochdorf and Saint-Denis discussed in Chapter 4, and in the use of visuality in feasting vessels and their arrangements in Hochdorf and Sutton Hoo. Even the adoption of Christianity does not seem to have had a major effect on the ways that visual structures were used. The woman's grave underneath Cologne cathedral is similar to many Iron Age burials with respect to the use of visual images. The Ardagh and Tassilo chalices, and the illuminated manuscripts of Lindisfarne and Kells, all use visuality in ways very similar to objects such as the Gundestrup cauldron and the Gallehus horns.

From these consistencies I would argue that this approach enables us to get at fundamentally important issues of perception and communication concerning ways that people use and respond to visual imagery. I have examined only a limited part of the world and only 1,400 years, and it would be interesting to expand this approach to other parts of the world and other periods.

Variations

Together with these general continuities, we can also identify variations over time. For example, the way that figurines were produced and finished changed. In the Early Iron Age (800-450 BC), bronze figurines of humans and of animals tended to be simple in execution, usually with smooth, untextured surfaces and with little by way of added incised features. The small horse figurines from the yoke at Hochdorf, the figurines on the Strettweg vehicle and many of the figurines from the site of Hallstatt are of this character. The large female figurine from Strettweg and the women holding up the Hochdorf couch have belts and some ring jewellery indicated, but they do not have the highly textured incising that we find on figurines of the succeeding period.

Early La Tène (450-350 BC) figurines, such as those on the Glauberg fibula, the Weiskirchen belt hook and the jugs from Basse-Yutz and the Dürrnberg, are characterised by a much greater degree of stylisation, with their very unnatural shapes (bulbous eyes and noses, spirals on limbs). Unlike the animals represented in the earlier period, now the creatures cannot always be identified with real animals. The human and animal images are often highly textured, with deeply incised lines covering much of their surfaces and often with colourful coral inlays.

In subsequent centuries, a new emphasis on incised two-dimensional representations is apparent, for example in decoration on scabbards. Three-dimensional figurines from the end of the prehistoric Iron Age and during the Roman Iron Age tend to be smoothly textured and realistic, with only limited use of incised lines as texturing features, as on the vulture head from Kelheim (Figure 3.3) and the human face from Vimose (Figure 6.2). In the latter part of the Roman Iron Age and in the early medieval period, we again find fantastic creatures and highly textured surfaces, as in Early La Tène contexts. As in the earlier period, these images are particularly common on fibulae and belt attachments, those objects situated in key positions on the body to attract the attention of others.

In studies of wealthy burials in different contexts, investigators have observed that exceptionally richly outfitted graves seem not so much to document the existence of great status differences in a society, but rather to indicate times of social and political upheaval, when competition for position and power results in extravagant funerary displays. The use of visually complex ornaments seems to follow a similar trajectory. The most elaborate figural ornament, in the Early La Tène period (Glauberg, Weiskirchen) and in early medieval times (Gallehus, Cologne, Saint-Denis, Donzdorf, Sutton Hoo), seems to have been used in times when political systems that had dominated for a period declined in their power (end of the Early Iron Age centres in the fifth century BC and with them the decline in the geometric style of ornament, decline of Roman power and rise of early medieval kingdoms in the fifth, sixth and seventh centuries AD). It is not my purpose here to explore connections between uses of visuality and changing cultural and political systems, but this line of inquiry is likely to be highly productive.

Responses

The archaeological evidence does not ordinarily give us a view into the immediate reactions and responses of early Europeans to the images that they saw. But we can assess their responses on a scale of years by examining ways in which they used other visually complex objects in the same regions at slightly later times.

Burials

Both the Hochdorf burial and that at Sutton Hoo were big events in their communities and in broader regional contexts. For Hochdorf, we are well informed about subsequent funerary practices in the same area. Hochdorf was part of the complex of burials around the Hohenasperg hilltop settlement, and it was among the earliest. We can be fairly certain that the funerary ritual practised on the occasion of the burial of the man at Hochdorf was long remembered by people who observed it and participated, and it is highly likely that the event was recalled in the oral traditions of the region for long after. Within a 10km radius of the Hohenasperg, 23 unusually large burial mounds have been identified, of which the Hochdorf tumulus is one. There were surely large numbers of more modest burials in this fertile region, many of which have been destroyed by agricultural activity and many of which remain to be discovered. In some of the large mounds, such as Grafenbühl and Kleinaspergle, archaeologists have excavated burials of a slightly later date than Hochdorf. Since all of these mounds represent ritual performances by the same population of the Hohenasperg region, we can assume that the funerary event at Hochdorf, including the laying out of the body with its colourful garments and its gold ornaments, the arrangement of feasting vessels in the different parts of the chamber and the wrapping of the grave contents in fabric just before closing the burial, were all recalled at the time of planning and performing these subsequent burials.

Both the Grafenbühl grave and the central burial in the Kleinaspergle tumulus were looted in antiquity, and thus a full assessment of the ways in which memories of the visual effects of the Hochdorf funeral were applied to these later graves is not possible. But in the Grafenbühl grave, remains of furniture suggest objects comparable to the couch at Hochdorf, and fragments of sheet gold missed by the looters indicate that textured gold ornaments were displayed here, as at Hochdorf. Bronze vessels were also part of the assemblage at Grafenbühl, but their fragmentary nature and the likelihood that others were carted off by the looters makes comparison with Hochdorf impossible.

At Kleinaspergle, the side chamber excavated at the end of the nineteenth century had arranged in it at least seven vessels of a feasting set. They included three bronze vessels, two Attic kylikes and two drinking horns, as well as pieces of textured sheet gold that may have been arranged on the body of the deceased in a fashion similar to that at Hochdorf; but here again, we lack a good plan of the grave.

Another way to assess response to the visual effects of the Hochdorf funeral is through the material culture associated with the majority of people. At a funeral on the scale of that of Hochdorf, we have to assume that large numbers of people from throughout the greater region witnessed the event. It is likely that people who did so wished to emulate some of what they saw in the great funeral display when the time came for them to perform funerals for members of their own families and communities. It is not likely that most people could get their hands on gold for ornaments, but they may well have desired to replicate some of what they saw in the bronze, iron or wooden ornaments to which they had access. To investigate this question, a detailed study of bronze belt plates and ring jewellery that was placed in graves in the region shortly after 540 BC (the date for Hochdorf) could produce enlightening results. It would also be interesting to see whether the inclusion of ceramic vessels in graves increased after the Hochdorf burial took place, and whether the placement of such vessels reflected responses to the Hochdorf ceremony.

Ritual

To judge responses to the uses of visually powerful imagery in ritual settings, again a potentially productive approach is to examine how images were used in subsequent contexts. As with the burial ceremonies discussed above, here again visually spectacular ritual events would remain vivid in the memories of the participants. Burning images on lake shores or hilltops at the *Brandopferplätze*, erecting them on the edges of ponds at Oberdorla and Forlev Nymølle, and throwing them into dark woodland pools at Illerup and Vimose – all done under conditions conducive to strong emotional participation on the part of observers – would have left vivid memories in their minds. Comparison with later practices in these rituals is more difficult than that for burials, because these events generally took place over extended periods of time rather than in a single ceremony. But it may be possible on the basis of stratigraphic evidence to compare progressive changes at Gournay and Illerup, for example, to judge the extent to which the visual memory of an earlier ceremony structured the performance of a later one.

Responses to the Christian chalices and the illuminated manuscripts can best be judged by examining texts written by church officials of the period. These objects were designed to provide people with emotional experiences of the new religion. Since many of the writings of the seventh and eighth centuries deal with the business of converting people to Christianity, this would be the best place to look for indications of responses to the visual qualities of these objects. The fact that church silver continued to be produced in similar style to the Ardagh and Tassilo chalices, and Lindisfarne was just the first of a series of such manuscripts, suggests that these visually potent objects elicited the responses desired by the church officials.

Landscape images

Responses to imagery created in landscapes are very difficult to assess, because the surface of the land has been changing continuously as communities put the land to new uses. Early recorded oral traditions about landscape features would be potential sources of information to examine. Traditional names of sites, such as Devils Dyke and Teufelsmauer, can be informative. Longstanding practices of maintenance of images in the landscape can inform us about how people responded to those images, as in the case of the Uffington White Horse. We can experience some of the landscape structures from early Europe directly today, such as surviving burial mounds, reconstructed tumuli and standing stones of early medieval times, such as the Irish High Crosses. But situated as they are in regions that are now populated much more densely than they were when they were erected, in landscapes that have been transformed by industrial processes, it is difficult to imagine the experiences of people in the visual world of which these images originally were parts.

Visual imagery and texts

During the entire period covered by this book, 600 BC-AD 800, the peoples with whom I have been concerned, while practising very little writing themselves, were in contact with people who did. From the sixth century BC on, Greek and other scripts appear in southern Gaul, and with the abundant evidence we have for interaction between elites of temperate Europe and communities along the Mediterranean coasts, there is no doubt that they were aware of writing as a technology. But while there are clear indications that some individuals made limited use of writing in pre-Roman temperate Europe, such as the sherds from Manching with Greek letters incised into them and the bronze tablet from Chamalières in France, there is no indication that any communities, or even any small elite groups, adopted writing as a practice in the pre-Roman Iron Age.

When local forms of writing do appear, the technology was used for only very limited purposes, and not to compose complex texts. Runes were developed, probably in or near what is now Denmark, during the first or second century AD, by one or more individuals who were familiar with the Latin script. In the early centuries of their use, runic inscriptions occur primarily on women's fibulae and on weapons. The inscriptions are short and generally concern the identity of the user or maker. The practice of inscribing objects with runes spread widely throughout Europe, but it remained a practice limited to a small elite group. When Latin inscriptions on local objects begin to appear in the fifth century, Klaus Düwel notes that runic inscriptions tend to be 'hidden' on the back of objects, while Latin inscriptions usually occur on the more publicly visible front. While a number of important texts survive from the latter centuries of our period, such as the writings of Gregory of Tours and Bede, the number of people who were literate was small. It was not until the end of the eighth century that concern with expanding the role of writing grew, and with it the establishment of church schools for the training of clergy.

A number of the later objects discussed in this book include both elements of visual complexity and early writing. On the back of the Donzdorf fibula is a runic inscription. Arnegunde's ring has her name written on it. And both chalices and the Lindisfarne manuscript combine complex visual imagery with texts of a specifically Christian nature. Such combinations raise particularly interesting questions about the relationships between these two modes of communication in the early medieval world.

Much recent scholarship on the subject of the adoption of writing suggests that when a society takes up this new technology of communication, great changes come about in people's consciousness. Writing constituted a way of making information and records permanent in a way that oral transmission did not, and writing could transmit information over distance, by transporting written documents. While I have no doubt that the development and the adoption of writing as a technology had powerful effects on thinking over the long term, I question whether the increase in the use of writing in our period had any profound significance in changing worldviews by the ninth century in more than a very small group of specialists. We tend to overestimate the immediate effects of writing because we cannot imagine a world without it. Writing was certainly important in the church and in monasteries, and it was gaining significance in political and cultural spheres as well, but for the vast majority of people, writing had little significance.

What are we missing?

Applying some of the new ideas that have arisen from neurobiological research and from investigations in the field of cognitive psychology to the use of visually complex objects in early Europe gives us a new way to think about why objects were fashioned the way they were, and why they were placed – in graves, on ritual sites, in the landscape – where they were. But we are only at the beginning of understanding some of the information that is embedded in the objects that people made, saw and responded to two millennia ago. Much still remains hidden from us, I believe, but can be discovered through future research. Interaction between the scientists who study how human visual perception works, and archaeologists who study objects from the past and the ways that people situated them within their visual worlds, holds great promise for the future.

Bibliographic essay

Preface
On the concept 'elites' see Pakulski 2006.

1. Image and response in Early Europe
Images, today and in the past
Images as a general issue: Mirzoeff 1999, Burke 2001, Mitchell 2005.

Images, their meaning and what they did (and do)
Gallehus horns: Brøndsted 1954. Iron Age art: Jacobsthal 1944. Meaning in early medieval animal ornament: Magnus 1997, Høilund Nielsen 1998. Political interpretation: Hedeager 2000. Mutability of meanings in imagery: Callmer 2006; also Zeki 1999. Viewer brings own meaning to images: Brilliant 1984: 15-20, Sacks 2004. Images as physical objects: Gell 1992.

Different ways of seeing
Human Image exhibit in London: King 2000. 'Classical ideal' as formative for our ideas about representation: Preziosi 1998: 21-2, Beard and Henderson 2001: 1-9. Dutch seventeenth-century landscapes as models: Adams 2002. Different ways of seeing: Berger 1972, Lowe 1982, Baxandall 1988, Deregowski 1989, Frank 2000: 103, Nelson 2000.

Changes in perceiving visually
Increased availability of images from fifteenth century: Smith 2004, McDonald 2005. Greater increase in nineteenth century: Anderson 1991, Lenman 2005.

The investigator's responses
Taking account of the investigator's responses to images: Zwijnenberg and Farago 2003: xi-xii, and to landscape phenomena: Ingold 2005.

145

Image and Response in Early Europe

The material: images in early Europe
Earliest images in Europe: Clottes 2003, Conard 2003. Bronze Age: Capelle 1974. Prehistoric Iron Age: Kossack 1954, Megaw and Megaw 1989, Huth 2003, Aldhouse-Green 2004. Roman Iron Age: Jørgensen et al. 2003. Early medieval period: Haseloff 1981, *Die Franken* 1996, Capelle 2003. Images north of Black Sea: Aruz et al. 2006. In East Asia: Yang 1999. Hochdorf: Biel 1985.

2. Vision, visuality, visual images

The physics of seeing
Gregory 1997, Zeki 1998, 1999, Ramachandran 2004.

Cognitive psychology of vision
Gombrich 1961. Conscious and unconscious vision: Wilson 2002, Goodale and Milner 2004, Searle 2006. Case of Mike May regaining vision: Kurson 2007. Scanning and fixation: Gregory 1997, Henderson 2003, Henderson and Castelhano 2005, Underwood 2005, Ogmen and Breitmeyer 2006. Cognitive map: Kandel 2006: 298. Seeing complex objects: Lindstrøm and Kristoffersen 2001, Livingstone 2002: 158. Fooling visual perceptions: Gombrich 1963, Gregory 1997: 47-50, Frith 2007: 43, Kurson 2007: 232-3. Gorilla story: Simons and Chabris 1999.

Images shape the mind
Freedberg 1989, Stafford 2007.

Visual and mental experience and structural change in the brain
Enlarged hippocampus in brains of London taxi drivers: Maguire et al. 2000. Thickened portions of cortex in meditaters: Bhattacharjee 2005.

Development and character of visual perception
Development of baby's visual familiarity with the world, in conjunction with handling objects: Gregory 1997: 250, Wexler 2006. Greater complexity to perceiving images than other things: Mitchell 2005.

Visuality in the past
Images available in the past: Muizelaar and Phillips 2003.

3. Structuring visuality

Structures of visuality
On surfaces and texture, see Gibson 1950, 1980, 1986. Edges or frames: Gregory 1997: 55-6, Ankersmit 2003, Brett 2005. Decoration:

Bibliographic essay

Riegl 1901-23, Gombrich 1984, Brett 2005. Colour: Jones and MacGregor 2002. Lighting: Ramachandran 1995.

Themes
Pictures: Gibson 1986, Mitchell 2005. Power of faces to stimulate the brain, and universality of facial expressions: Ekman 1982, Bruce and Green 1990, Perrett et al. 1995, Bruce and Young 1998, Zeki 1999: 167-79, Muizelaar and Phillips 2003: 4, van de Vall 2003, Goodale and Milner 2004: 59, Kandel 2006: 386; Pease and Pease 2006. Eyes and mouth as special elements of face in visually perceiving: Gregory 1997: 74. Shape referencing: Fitzpatrick 2007; Gommern: Becker 2000.

Enhancing visuality
Techniques applied: Roth 1986, Megaw and Megaw 1989.

Encounters
Emotional responses to images: Freedberg 1989, Damasio 2003. 'Technologies of enchantment' were outlined by Gell 1992, 1998, applied by Williams 2006: 141. Donzdorf: Neuffer 1972. Bifrons: Haseloff 1981: 47, fig. 25. Visual puzzles: Leigh 1984, Ramachandran 2004.

The visual world of early Europeans
Concept of the 'visual world'; Gibson 1950. Photograph of interior of reconstructed Iron Age house: Kreuz 2002: 75, fig. 47.

Some responses to images from early Europe
Hochdorf: Biel 1985. Apahida: Harhoiu 2007. Sutton Hoo buckle: Bruce-Mitford 1978.

4. Images for individuals

Ornaments worn on the body
Belt plates: Kilian-Dirlmeier 1972. Hochdorf gold: Biel 1985; textiles: Banck 1996. Glauberg fibula: Frey 2002a. Weiskirchen belt hook: Megaw 1970, nr. 62. Chessel Down: Dalton 1923: 30, fig. 22. Donzdorf: Neuffer 1972. Sutton Hoo buckle: Bruce-Mitford 1978, Marzinzik 2006. Saint-Denis: Fleury and France-Lanord 1998.

Carrying ornaments
La Tène sword scabbards: Keller 1866, de Navarro 1972. Apahida 2: Horedt and Protase 1972, Harhoiu 2007.

Reshaping the body
Artificial shaping of the skull: Schröter 1988, Teschler-Nicola and

147

Mitteröcker 2007. 'Swebian knot' represented on bronze figurines and in hair of bog bodies: Krierer 2002. Personal care implements in Late Iron Age and Roman Period find contexts: Hill 1997, Crummy and Eckardt 2003.

5. Images for the group

Vessels: pottery and communal consumption
Iron Age pottery discussed here: Hoernes 1891, Zürn 1957.

Feasts and funerals
Feasts: Dietler and Hayden 2001. Early Iron Age feasts: Kossack 1964, 1970, Arnold 1999.

Hochdorf and its feasting assemblage
Hochdorf: Biel 1985, 1996. Vessels: Krausse 1996, Bieg 2002. Textiles: Banck 1996, Banck-Burgess 1999. Situla scenes: Kastelic 1965.

The Basse-Yutz jugs
Megaw and Megaw 1990.

Sutton Hoo feasting
Sutton Hoo: Bruce-Mitford 1978, Carver 1998, 2005, Willliams 2006. Textiles: Crowfoot 1983.

Mass production of images: Iron Age coins
Allen and Nash 1980, Haselgrove and Wigg-Wolf 2005.

6. Images for magic and religion

Magical properties of manufactured objects: Hingley 1997, 2006; Blakely 2006; Giles 2007; of images especially: Mitchell 2005. Magic permeates material life: Wilson 2000.

Amulets
Hansemann and Kriss-Rettenbeck 1977; Pauli 1975. Gündlingen: Dehn 1994. Small human figures as amulets in graves: Zürn 1970: plate M, A2, Keller 1965: plate 26a and b, 19.20, plate 29. Simleul Silvaniei gold chain: Zhuber-Okrog 2007. Bracteates: Hauck 1992.

Ritual places
Open-air sites: Brunaux 1999, Lambot and Méniel 2000, Arcelin and Brunaux 2003, Poux 2006. Displays: fire: Zanier 1999. Displays: water: Torbrügge 1971, Bradley 1998. Oberdorla: Behm-Blancke 2002.

Wooden images: Capelle 1995, van der Sanden and Capelle 2002. Quotation from Kaul 2003: 34. Illerup: Ilkjaer 2003.

Vessels for ritual
Vessels and religious ritual: Davidson 1988, Green 1998. Gundestrup: Kaul 1995. Gallehus: Brøndsted 1954. Ardagh chalice: Mitchell 1977, Richardson 2005. Tassilo chalice: Haseloff 1951.

Cologne woman's grave
Doppelfeld 1960. Analysis of fibulae: von Carnap-Bornheim 1996. Interpreting Anglo-Saxon ornament: Webster 2003.

Illuminated manuscripts
Lindisfarne: Backhouse 1981.

7. Images in landscapes

Landscapes as surfaces
Gibson 1950, 1986. As active embodiments of the human past: Chapman and Gearey 2000, Thomas 2006.

Landscapes as backgrounds
Mitchell 2002.

Landscape and memory
Schama 1995, Barrett 1999, Tilley 2004, Ingold 2005, Holtorf and Williams 2006.

Sculptured stones of the Iron Age
Frey 2002b, Bonenfant and Guillaumet 1998, Rolle 2006. Vix statues: Chaume and Reinhard 2002. Hirschlanden: Zürn 1970. Possibility of painted colours on statues: Barbet 1991, Frey 2002b; see also Brinkmann and Wurnig 2004. Glauberg earthworks: Herrmann 2002.

Halls
Hall at Gudme: Michaelsen and Sørensen 1993; Uppåkra: Larsson and Lenntorp 2004, Larsson 2006; Yeavering: Hope-Taylor 1977. See also Newman 2007. Charlemagne's chapel and hall complex: Boussard 1968.

High Crosses of Ireland
Richardson and Scarry 1990, Harbison 1994. Ogham stones: Charles-Edwards 2000.

Uffington White Horse
Hughes 1859, Barclay et al. 2003, Gosden and Lock 2007.

8. Images and visuality

Vision and visual enhancement
Organisation of craft production: Roth 1986, Wells 2007. München-Perlach: Reimann and Bartel 2001. Christo's wrapping: Chiappini 2006.

Continuities and variations of visual representation
Strettweg: Egg 1996. Hallstatt: Kromer 1959.

Responses
Other graves in Hochdorf region: Zürn 1970, Kimmig 1988.

Visual imagery and texts
Early writing in Europe: Feugère and Lambert 2004. Runes and early medieval Latin: Düwel 1997, Stoklund 2003. Writing and cognitive change: Ong 1982, Moreland 2006.

Bibliography

Adams, A.J. (2002), 'Competing communities in the "Great Bog of Europe": identity and seventeenth-century Dutch landscape painting', in Mitchell: 35-76.

Aldhouse-Green, M. (2004), *An Archaeology of Images: Iconology and Cosmology in Iron Age and Roman Europe* (London: Routledge).

Allen, D.F. and Nash, D. (1980), *The Coins of the Ancient Celts* (Edinburgh: Edinburgh University Press).

Anderson, P.J. (1991), *The Printed Image and the Transformation of Popular Culture 1790-1860* (Oxford: Clarendon Press).

Andrén, A., Jennbert, K. and Raudvere, C. (eds) (2006), *Old Norse Religion in Long-Term Perspectives* (Lund: Nordic Academic Press).

Anke, B. and Externbrink, H. (eds) (2007), *Attila und die Hunnen* (Speyer: Historisches Museum der Pfalz).

Ankersmit, F.R. (2003), 'Rococo as the dissipation of boredom', in Farago and Zwijnenberg (eds): 112-31.

Arcelin, P. and Brunaux, J.-L. (eds) (2003), 'Cultes et sanctuaires en France à l'âge du Fer', *Gallia* 60: 1-268.

Arnold, B. (1999), '"Drinking the feast": alcohol and the legitimation of power in Celtic Europe', *Cambridge Archaeological Journal* 9: 71-93.

Aruz, J., Farkas, A. and Fino, E.V. (eds) (2006), *The Golden Deer of Eurasia: Perspectives on the Steppe Nomads of the Ancient World* (New York: The Metropolitan Museum of Art).

Backhouse, J. (1981), *The Lindisfarne Gospels* (London: Phaidon).

Baitinger, H. and Pinsker, B. (eds) (2002), *Das Rätsel der Kelten vom Glauberg* (Stuttgart: Konrad Theiss Verlag).

Banck, J. (1996), 'Spinnen, webe, färben: feine Tuche für den Fürsten', in Biel (ed.): 40-63.

Banck-Burgess, J. (1999), *Hochdorf IV: Die Textilfunde aus dem späthallstattzeitlichen Fürstengrab von Eberdingen-Hochdorf (Kreis Ludwigsburg) und weitere Grabtextilien aus hallstatt- und latènezeitlichen Kulturgruppen* (Stuttgart: Konrad Theiss Verlag).

151

Bibliography

Barbet, A. (1991), 'Roquepertuse et la polychromie en Gaule méridionale à l'époque préromaine', *Documents d'Archéologie Mérionale* 14: 53-81.

Barclay, A., Cromarty, A.M., Gosden, C., Lock, G., Miles, D., Pamer, S. and Robinson, M. (2003), 'The White Horse and its landscape', in D. Miles et al., *Uffington White Horse and Its Landscape: Investigations at White Horse Hill, Uffington, 1989-95, and Tower Hill, Ashbury, 1993-4* (Oxford: Oxford Archaeology): 243-68.

Barrett, J.C. (1999), 'The mythical landscapes of the British Iron Age', in W. Ashmore and A.B. Knapp (eds), *Archaeologies of Landscape* (Oxford: Blackwell): 253-65.

Baxandall, M. (1988), *Painting and Experience in Fifteenth Century Italy* (2nd edn) (Oxford: Oxford University Press).

Beard, M. and Henderson, J. (2001), *Classical Art: From Greece to Rome* (Oxford: Oxford University Press).

Becker, M. (2000), 'Bekleidung-Schmuck-Ausrüstung', in S. Fröhlich (ed.), *Gold für die Ewigkeit: Das germanische Fürstengrab von Gommern* (Halle: Landesamt für Archäologie Sachsen-Anhalt): 127-47.

Behm-Blancke, G. (2002), *Heiligtümer der Germanen und ihrer Vorgänger in Thüringen: Die Kultstätte Oberdorla* (2 vols) (Stuttgart: Konrad Theiss Verlag).

Benjamin, W.B. (1968), *Illuminations* (trans. by H. Zohn) (New York: Harcourt Brace Jovanovich): 217-52.

Berger, J. (1972), *Ways of Seeing* (London: Penguin).

Bhattacharjee, Y. (2005), 'Neuroscientists welcome Dalai Lama with mostly open arms', *Science* 310, 5751: 1104.

Bieg, G. (2002), *Hochdorf V: Der Bronzekessel aus dem späthallstattzeitlichen Fürstengrab von Eberdingen-Hochdorf (Kreis Ludwigsburg)* (Stuttgart: Konrad Theiss Verlag).

Biel, J. (1985), *Der Keltenfürst von Hochdorf* (Stuttgart: Konrad Theiss Verlag).

Biel, J. (ed.) (1996), *Experiment Hochdorf: Keltische Handwerkskunst Wiederbelebt* (Stuttgart: Keltenmuseum Hochdorf/Enz).

Blakely, S. (2006), *Myth, Ritual, and Metallurgy in Ancient Greece and Recent Africa* (Cambridge: Cambridge University Press).

Bonenfant, P.-P. and Guillaumet, J.-P. (1998), *La statuaire anthropomorphe du premier âge du Fer* (Besançon: Edition de l'Université de Franche-Comté).

Boussard, J. (1968), *The Civilization of Charlemagne* (trans. by F. Partridge) (New York: McGraw-Hill).

Bibliography

Bradley, R. (1998), *The Passage of Arms: An Archaeological Analysis of Prehistoric Hoard and Votive Deposits* (2nd edn) (Oxford: Oxbow).

Brett, D. (2005), *Rethinking Decoration: Pleasure and Ideology in the Visual Arts* (Cambridge: Cambridge University Press).

Brilliant, R. (1984), *Visual Narratives: Storytelling in Etruscan and Roman Art* (Ithaca, NY: Cornell University Press).

Brinkmann, V. and Wurnig, U. (eds) (2004), *Bunte Götter: Die Farbigkeit antiker Skulptur* (Munich: Glyptothek).

Brøndsted, J. (1954), *Guldhornene* (Copenhagen: Nationalmuseet).

Bruce, V. and Green, P.R. (1990), *Visual Perception: Physiology, Psychology and Ecology* (2nd edn) (London: Lawrence Erlbaum Associates).

Bruce, V. and Young, A. (1998), *In the Eye of the Beholder: The Science of Face Perception* (Oxford: Oxford University Press).

Bruce-Mitford, R. (1978), 'The great gold buckle', in *The Sutton Hoo Ship-Burial*, vol. 2: *Arms, Armour and Regalia* (London: British Museum Press): 536-64.

Brunaux, J.-L. (1999), 'Ribemont-sur-Ancre (Somme)', *Gallia* 56: 177-283.

Burke, P. (2001), *Eyewitnessing: The Uses of Images as Historical Evidence* (London: Reaktion Books).

Callmer, J. (2006), 'Ornaments, ornamentation, and female gender: women in eastern central Sweden in the eighth and early ninth centuries', in Andrén et al.: 189-94.

Capelle, T. (1974), *Kunst und Kunsthandwerk im bronzezeitlichen Nordeuropa* (Neumünster: K. Wachholtz).

Capelle, T. (1995), *Anthropomorphe Holzidole in Mittel- und Nordeuropa* (Stockholm: Almqvist & Wiksell).

Capelle, T. (2003), *Die verborgenen Menschen in der germanischen Ornamentkunst des frühen Mittelalters* (Stockholm: Almqvist & Wiksell).

Carnap-Bornheim, C. von. (1996), 'Zoomorphes Cloisonné auf dem Bügelfibelpaar aus dem Frauengrab unter dem Kölner Dom', *Archäologisches Korrespondenzblatt* 26: 507-16.

Carver, M. (1998), *Sutton Hoo: Burial Ground of Kings?* (London: British Museum Press).

Carver, M. (2005), *Sutton Hoo: A Seventh-Century Princely Burial Ground and its Context* (London: British Museum Press).

Chapman, H.P. and Gearey, B.R. (2000), 'Palaeoecology and the perception of prehistoric landscapes: some comments on visual approaches to phenomenology', *Antiquity* 74: 316-19.

Bibliography

Charles-Edwards, T.M. (2000), *Early Christian Ireland* (Cambridge: Cambridge University Press).

Chaume, B. and Reinhard, W. (2002), 'Das frühkeltische Heiligtum von Vix', in Baitinger and Pinsker (eds): 221-2.

Chiappini, R. (ed.) (2006), *Christo and Jeanne-Claude* (Lugano: Museo d'Arte Moderna).

Clottes, J. (2003), *Chauvet Cave: The Art of Earliest Times* (trans. by P. Bahn) (Salt Lake City, UT: University of Utah Press).

Conard, N. (2003), 'Palaeolithic ivory sculptures from southwestern Germany and the origins of figurative art', *Nature* 426: 830-32.

Crowfoot, E. (1983), 'The textiles', in A.C. Evans (ed.), *The Sutton Hoo Ship-Burial*, vol. 3 (London: British Museum Press): 409-79.

Crummy, N. and Eckardt, H. (2003), 'Regional identities and technologies of the self: nail-cleaners in Roman Britain', *Archaeological Journal* 160: 44-69.

Dalton, O.M. (1923), *A Guide to the Anglo-Saxon and Foreign Teutonic Antiquities in the Department of British and Medieval Antiquities* (London: British Museum Press).

Damasio, A. (2003), *Looking for Spinoza: Joy, Sorrow, and the Feeling Brain* (London: Harcourt).

Darwin, C. (1872), *The Expression of the Emotions in Man and Animals* (London: John Murray).

Davidson, H.R.E. (1988), *Myths and Symbols in Pagan Europe: Early Scandinavian and Celtic Religions* (Syracuse, NY: Syracuse University Press).

Déchelette, J. (1913), *Manuel d'archéologie préhistorique, celtique et gallo-romaine. II: Archéologie celtique ou protohistorique. Part 2: Premier âge du Fer ou époque de Hallstatt* (Paris: Auguste Picard).

Dehn, R. (1994), 'Das Grab einer "besonderen Frau" der Frühlatènezeit von Gündlingen, Stadt Breisach, Kreis Breisgau-Hochschwarzwald', *Archäologische Ausgrabungen in Baden-Württemberg 1994:* 92-94.

Deregowski, J.B. (1989), 'Real space and represented space: cross-cultural perspectives', *Behavioral and Brain Sciences* 12: 51-119.

Dietler, M. and Hayden, B. (eds) (2001), *Feasts: Archaeological and Ethnographic Perspectives on Food, Politics, and Power* (Washington, DC: Smithsonian Institution Press).

Doppelfeld, O. (1960), 'Das fränkische Frauengrab unter dem Chor des Kölner Domes', *Germania* 38: 89-113.

Düwel, K. (1997), 'Frühe Schriften bei den Barbaren: Germanische Runen, lateinische Inschriften', in K. Fuchs et al., *Die Alamannen* (Stuttgart: Archäologisches Landesmuseum): 491-8.

Bibliography

Egg, M. (1996), *Das hallstattzeitliche Fürstengrab von Strettweg bei Judenburg in der Obersteiermark* (Mainz: Römisch-Germanisches Zentralmuseum).

Ekman, P. (1982), *Emotion in the Human Face* (New York: Cambridge University Press).

Engelhardt, C. (1863), *Thorsbjerg Mosefund* (Copenhagen: G. Klingsey and Thieles Bogtrykkeri).

Engelhardt, C. (1866), *Denmark in the Early Iron Age* (London: Williams and Norgate).

Engelhardt, C. (1867), *Om Vimose-Fundet* (Copenhagen: Thieles Bogtrykkeri).

Engelhardt, C. (1869), *Vimose Fundet* (Copenhagen: Thieles Bogtrykkeri).

Farago, C. and Zwijnenberg, R. (eds) (2003), *Compelling Visuality: The Work of Art in and out of History* (Minneapolis, MN: University of Minnesota Press).

Feugère, M. and Lambert, P.-Y. (2004), 'L'écriture dans la société gallo-romaine', *Gallia* 61: 1-192.

Fitzpatrick, A.P. (2007), 'Dancing with dragons: fantastic animals in the earlier Celtic art of Iron Age Britain', in C. Haselgrove and T. Moore (eds), *The Later Iron Age in Britain and Beyond* (Oxford: Oxbow): 339-57.

Fleury, M. and France-Lanord, A. (1998), *Les trésors mérovingiens de la basilique de Saint-Denis* (Woippy: Gérard Klopp).

Frank, G. (2000), *The Memory of the Eyes: Pilgrims to Living Saints in Christian Late Antiquity* (London: University of California Press).

Die Franken: Wegbereiter Europas (1996) (Mainz: Philipp von Zabern).

Freedberg, D. (1989), *The Power of Images: Studies in the History and Theory of Response* (London: University of Chicago Press).

Frey, O.-H. (2002a), 'Frühe keltische Kunst: Dämonen und Götter', in Baitinger and Pinsker (eds): 186-205.

Frey, O.-H. (2002b), 'Menschen oder Heroen? Die Statuen vom Glauberg und die frühe keltische Grossplastik', in Baitinger and Pinsker (eds): 208-18.

Frey, O.-H. (2002c), 'Die Fürstengräber vom Glauberg', in Baitinger and Pinsker (eds): 172-85.

Frith, C. (2007), *Making up the Mind: How the Brain Creates our Mental World* (Oxford: Blackwell).

Gell, A. (1992), 'The technology of enchantment and the enchantment of technology', in J. Coote and A. Shelton (eds), *Anthropology, Art and Aesthetics* (Oxford: Clarendon Press): 40-63.

Bibliography

Gell, A. (1998), *Art and Agency: An Anthropological Theory* (Oxford: Clarendon Press).

Gibson, J.J. (1950), *The Perception of the Visual World* (Boston, MA: Houghton Mifflin).

Gibson, J.J. (1980), 'A prefatory essay on the perception of surfaces versus the perception of markings on a surface', in M.A. Hagen (ed.), *The Perception of Pictures*, vol. 1 (New York: Academic Press): xi-xvii.

Gibson, J.J. 1986. *The Ecological Approach to Visual Perception*. London: Lawrence Erlbaum Associates.

Giles, M. (2007), 'Making metal and forging relations: ironworking in the British Iron Age', *Oxford Journal of Archaeology* 26: 395-413.

Gombrich, E.H. (1961), *Art and Illusion: A Study in the Psychology of Pictorial Representation* (2nd edn) (Princeton, NJ: Princeton University Press).

Gombrich, E. (1963), 'Illusion and visual deadlock', in *Meditations on a Hobby Horse and Other Essays on the Theory of Art* (Chicago, IL: University of Chicago Press): 151-61.

Gombrich, E.H. (1984), *The Sense of Order: A Study in the Psychology of Decorative Art* (Ithaca, NY: Cornell University Press).

Goodale, M.A. and Milner, A.D. (2004), *Sight Unseen: An Exploration of Conscious and Unconscious Vision* (Oxford: Oxford University Press).

Gosden, C. and Lock, G. (2007), 'The aesthetics of landscape on the Berkshire Downs', in C. Haselgrove and R. Pope (eds), *The Earlier Iron Age in Britain and the Near Continent* (Oxford: Oxbow): 279-92.

Green, M.J. (1998), 'Vessels of death: sacred cauldrons in archaeology and myth', *Antiquaries Journal* 78: 63-84.

Gregory, R.L. (1997), *Eye and Brain: The Psychology of Seeing* (5th edn) (Oxford: Oxford University Press).

Gregory, R., Harris, J., Heard, P. and Rose, D. (eds) (1995), *The Artful Eye* (Oxford: Oxford University Press).

Haffner, A. (1976), *Die westliche Hunsrück-Eifel-Kultur* (Berlin: Walter de Gruyter).

Hansemann, L. and Kriss-Rettenbeck, L. (1977), *Amulett und Talisman: Erscheinungsform und Geschichte* (Munich: Georg D.W. Callwey).

Harbison, P. (1994), *Irish High Crosses* (Drogheda: Boyne Valley Honey Company).

Harhoiu, R. (2007), 'Hunnen und Germanen an der unteren Donau', in Anke and Externbrink (eds): 83-93.

Bibliography

Haselgrove, C. and Wigg-Wolf, D. (eds) (2005), *Iron Age Coinage and Ritual Practices* (Mainz: Philipp von Zabern).

Haseloff, G. (1951), *Der Tassilokelch* (Munich: C.H. Beck).

Haseloff, G. (1981), *Die germanische Tierornamentik der Völkerwanderungszeit* (3 vols) (Berlin: Walter de Gruyter).

Hauck, K. (1992), 'Frühmittalterliche Bildüberlieferung und der organisierte Kult (Zur Ikonologie der Goldbrakteaten XLIV)', in K. Hauck (ed.), *Der historische Horizont der Götterbild-Amulette aus der Übergangsepoche von der Spät-Antike zum frühen Mittelalter* (Göttingen: Vandenhoeck & Ruprecht): 435-574.

Hedeager, L. (2000), 'Migration period Europe: the formation of a political mentality', in F. Theuws and J.L. Nelson (eds), *Rituals of Power from Late Antiquity to the Early Middle Ages* (Leiden: Brill): 15-57.

Henderson, J.M. (2003), 'Human gaze control during real-world scene perception', *Trends in Cognitive Sciences* 7, 11: 498-504.

Henderson, J.M. and Castelhano, M.S. (2005), 'Eye movements and visual memory for scenes', in Underwood: 213-35.

Herrmann, F.-R. (2002), 'Der Glauberg: Fürstensitz, Fürstengräber und Heiligtum', in Baitinger and Pinsker (eds): 90-107.

Hill, J.D. (1997), '"The end of one kind of body and the beginning of another kind of body?" Toilet instruments and Romanization', in A. Gwilt and C. Haselgrove (eds), *Reconstructing Iron Age Societies* (Oxford: Oxbow): 96-107.

Hingley, R. (1997), 'Iron, ironworking and regeneration: a study of the symbolic meaning of metalworking in Iron Age Britain', in A. Gwilt and C. Haselgrove (eds), *Reconstructing Iron Age Societies* (Oxford: Oxbow): 9-18.

Hingley, R. (2006), 'The deposition of iron objects during the later prehistoric and Roman periods: contextual analysis and the significance of iron', *Britannia* 37: 213-57.

Hoernes, M. (1891), 'Ausgrabungen bei Oedenburg', *Mitteilungen der Anthropologischen Gesellschaft in Wien* 21, Sitzungsberichte: 71-8.

Høilund Nielsen, K. (1998), 'Animal style – a symbol of might and myth: Salin's style II in a European context', *Acta Archaeologica* 69: 1-52.

Holtorf, C. and Williams, H. (2006), 'Landscapes and memories', in D. Hicks and M.C. Beaudry (eds), *The Cambridge Companion to Historical Archaeology* (Cambridge: Cambridge University Press): 235-54.

Hope-Taylor, B. (1977), *Yeavering: An Anglo-British Centre of Early Northumbria* (London: HM Stationery Office).

Bibliography

Horedt, K. and Protase, D. (1972), 'Das zweite Fürstengrab von Apahida (Siebenbürgen)', *Germania* 50: 174-220.

Hughes, T. (1859), *The Scouring of the White Horse* (Cambridge: Macmillan).

Huth, C. (2003), *Menschenbilder und Menschenbild: Anthropomorphe Bildwerke der frühen Eisenzeit* (Berlin: Dietrich Reimer Verlag).

Ilkjaer, J. (2003), 'Danish war booty sacrifices', in Jørgensen et al. (eds): 44-65.

Ingold, T. (2005), 'Landscape lives, but archaeology turns to stone', *Norwegian Archaeological Review* 38: 122-9.

Jacobsthal, P. (1934), 'Einige Werke keltischer Kunst', *Die Antike* 10: 17-45.

Jacobsthal, P. (1944), *Early Celtic Art* (2 vols) (Oxford: Clarendon Press).

Jones, A. and MacGregor, G. (eds) (2002), *Colouring the Past: The Significance of Colour in Archaeological Research* (Oxford: Berg).

Jørgensen, L., Storgaard, B. and Thomsen, L.G. (eds) (2003), *The Spoils of Victory: The North in the Shadow of the Roman Empire* (Copenhagen: National Museum).

Kandel, E.R. (2006), *In Search of Memory: The Emergence of a New Science of Mind* (New York: W.W. Norton).

Kastelic, J. (1965), *Situla Art* (New York: McGraw-Hill).

Kaul, F. (1995), 'The Gundestrup cauldron reconsidered', *Acta Archaeologica* 66: 1-38.

Kaul, F. (2003), 'The bog – the gateway to another world', in Jørgensen et al. (eds): 18-43.

Keller, F. (1866), *The Lake Dwellings of Switzerland and Other Parts of Europe* (trans. by J.E. Lee) (London: Longman, Green and Co).

Keller, J. (1965), *Das keltische Fürstengrab von Reinheim* (Mainz: Römisch-Germanisches Zentralmuseum).

Kilian-Dirlmeier, I. (1972), *Die hallstattzeitlichen Gürtelbleche und Blechgürtel Mitteleuropas* (Munich: C.H. Beck).

Kimmig, W. (ed.) (1988), *Das Kleinaspergle* (Stuttgart: Konrad Theiss).

King, J.C.H. (2000), *Human Image* (London: British Museum Press).

Kossack, G. (1954), *Studien zum Symbolgut der Urnenfelder- und Hallstattzeit Mitteleuropas* (Berlin: Walter de Gruyter).

Kossack, G. (1964), 'Trinkgeschirr als Kultgerät der Hallstattzeit', in P. Grimm (ed.), *Varia Archaeologica* (Berlin: Deutsche Akademie der Wissenschaften): 96-105.

Kossack, G. (1970), *Gräberfelder der Hallstattzeit an Main und Fränkischer Saale* (Kallmünz: Michael Lassleben).

Bibliography

Krausse, D. (1996): *Hochdorf III: Das Trink- und Speiseservice aus dem späthallstattzeitlichen Fürstengrab von Eberdingen-Hochdorf (Kreis Ludwigsburg)* (Stuttgart: Konrad Theiss Verlag).

Kreuz, A. (2002), 'Landwirtschaft und Umwelt im keltischen Hessen', in Baitinger and Pinsker (eds): 75-89.

Krierer, K.R. (2002), 'Germanenbüsten auf dem Kessel: Die Henkelattaschen des Bronzekessels', in J. Peska and J. Tejral (eds), *Das germanische Königsgrab von Mušov in Mähren*, vol. 2 (Mainz: Römisch-Germanisches Zentralmuseum): 367-85.

Kromer, K. (1959), *Das Gräberfeld von Hallstatt* (Florence: Sansoni).

Kurson, R. (2007), *Crashing Through: A True Story of Risk, Adventure, and the Man Who Dared to See* (New York: Random House).

Lambot, B. and Méniel, P. (2000), 'Le centre communautaire et cultuel du village gaulois d'Acy-Romance dans son contexte régional', in S. Verger (ed.), *Rites et espaces en pays celte et méditerranéen* (Rome: École française de Rome): 7-139.

Larsson, L. (2006), 'Ritual building and ritual space', in Andrén et al. (eds): 248-53.

Larsson, L. and Lenntorp, K.-M. (2004), 'The enigmatic house', in L. Larsson (ed.), *Continuity for Centuries: A Ceremonial Building and its Context at Uppåkra, Southern Sweden* (Stockholm: Almqvist & Wiksell International): 3-48.

Leigh, D. (1984), 'Ambiguity in Anglo-Saxon art', *Antiquaries Journal* 64: 34-42.

Lenman, R. (ed.) (2005), *The Oxford Companion to the Photograph* (Oxford: Oxford University Press).

Lindstrøm, T.C. and Kristoffersen, S. (2001), '"Figure it out!" Psychological perspectives on perception in Migration period animal art', *Norwegian Archaeological Review* 34: 65-84.

Livingstone, M. (2002), *Vision and Art: The Biology of Seeing* (New York: Harry N. Abrams).

Lowe, D.M. (1982), *History of Bourgeois Perception* (London: University of Chicago Press).

McDonald, M.P. (2005), 'Printmaking and print collecting in the Renaissance', in *Ferdinand Columbus: Renaissance Collector (1488-1539)* (London: British Museum Press): 15-32.

Magnus, B. (1997), 'The firebed of the serpent: myth and religion in the Migration period mirrored through some golden objects', in L. Webster and M. Brown (eds), *The Transformation of the Roman World AD 400-900* (Berkeley, CA: University of California Press): 194-207.

Bibliography

Maguire, E.A. et al. (2000), 'Navigation-related structural change in the hippocampi of taxi drivers', *Proceedings of the National Academy of Sciences* 97, 8: 4398-403.

Marzinzik, S. (2006), ' "De cingulis" – of belts and buckles in the Early Medieval period', *Saxon* 44: 1-2.

Megaw, J.V.S. (1970), *Art of the European Iron Age: A Study of the Elusive Image* (Bath: Adams & Dart).

Megaw, R. and V. (1989), *Celtic Art: From its Beginnings to the Book of Kells* (London: Thames and Hudson).

Megaw, V. and Megaw, R. (1990), *The Basse-Yutz Find: Masterpieces of Celtic Art* (London: Society of Antiquaries).

Michaelsen, K.K. and Sørensen, P.Ø. (1993), 'En kongsgård fra jernalderen', *Årbog for Svendborg & Omegns Museum 1993*: 24-35.

Mirzoeff, N. (1999), *An Introduction to Visual Culture* (London: Routledge).

Mitchell, G.F. (1977), 'Catalogue entries', in P. Cone (ed.), *Treasures of Early Irish Art 1500 BC to 1500 AD* (New York: Metropolitan Museum of Art).

Mitchell, W.J.T. (2002), 'Preface to the Second Edition', in Mitchell (ed.): vii-xii.

Mitchell, W.J.T. (ed.) (2002), *Landscape and Power* (2nd edn) (London: University of Chicago Press).

Mitchell, W.J.T. (2005), *What Do Pictures Want? The Lives and Loves of Images* (London: University of Chicago Press).

Montelius, O. (1869), *Från Jernåldern* (Stockholm: Iwar Haeggströms Boktryckeri).

Montelius, O. (1905), *Om Lifvet i Sverige under Hednatiden* (Stockholm: P.A. Norstedt & Söners Förlag).

Moreland, J. (2006), 'Archaeology and texts: subservience or enlightenment', *Annual Review of Anthropology* 35: 135-228.

Muizelaar, K. and Phillips, D. (2003), *Picturing Men and Women in the Dutch Golden Age: Paintings and People in Historical Perspective* (New Haven, CT: Yale University Press).

Navarro, J.M. de (1972), *The Finds from the Site of La Tène*: vol. 1: *Scabbards and the Swords Found in Them* (London: Oxford University Press).

Nelson, R.S. (2000), *Visuality Before and Beyond the Renaissance: Seeing as Others Saw* (Cambridge: Cambridge University Press).

Neuffer, E.M. (1972), *Der Reihengräberfriedhof von Donzdorf (Kreis Göppingen)* (Stuttgart: Müller & Gräff).

Newman, C. (2007), 'Procession and symbolism at Tara: analysis of

Bibliography

Tech Midchúarta (The "Banqueting Hall") in the context of the sacral campus', *Oxford Journal of Archaeology* 26: 415-38.

Ogmen, H. and Breitmeyer, B.G. (eds) (2006), *The First Half Second: The Microgenesis and Temporal Dynamics of Unconscious and Conscious Visual Processes* (London: MIT Press).

Ong, W.J. (1982), *Orality and Literacy: The Technologizing of the Word* (London: Methuen).

Pakulski, J. (2006), 'Elite(s)', in B.S. Turner (ed.), *The Cambridge Dictionary of Sociology* (Cambridge: Cambridge University Press): 162-3.

Pauli, L. (1975), *Keltische Volksglaube: Amulette und Sonderbestattungen am Dürrnberg bei Hallein und im eisenzeitlichen Mitteleuropa* (Munich: C.H. Beck).

Pease, A. and Pease, B. (2006), *The Definitive Book of Body Language* (New York: Bantam Dell).

Perrett, D., Benson, P.J., Hietnanen, J.K., Oram, M.W. and Dittrich, W.H. (1995), 'When is a face not a face?', in Gregory et al. (eds): 95-124.

Poux, M. (2006), 'Religion et société à l'âge du Fer: systèmes (en)clos et logiques rituelles', in C. Haselgrove (ed.), *Les Mutations de la Fin de l'Âge du Fer* (Glux-en-Glenne: Collection Bibracte): 181-99.

Preziosi, D. (ed.) (1998), *The Art of Art History: A Critical Anthology* (Oxford: Oxford University Press).

Ramachandran, V.S. (1995), '2-D or not 2-D – that is the question', in Gregory et al. (eds): 249-67.

Ramachandran, V.S. (2004), *A Brief Tour of Human Consciousness* (New York: Pi Press).

Reimann, D. and Bartel, A. (2001), 'Fibel und Futteral: München-Perlach Grab 18', *Bericht der bayerischen Bodendenkmalpflege* 41/42: 187-94.

Richardson, H. (2005), 'Visual arts and society', in D. Ó Cróinín (ed.), *A New History of Ireland,* vol. 1: *Prehistoric and Early Ireland* (Oxford: Oxford University Press): 680-713.

Richardson, H. and Scarry, J. (1990), *An Introduction to Irish High Crosses* (Dublin: Mercier Press).

Riegl, A. (1901-23), *Die spätrömische Kunstindustrie* (Vienna: K.K. Hof- und Staatsdruckerei).

Rolle, R. (2006), 'Royal tombs and hill fortresses: new perspectives on Scythian life', in J. Aruz, A. Farkas and E.V. Fino (eds), *The Golden Deer of Eurasia: Perspectives on the Steppe Nomads of the Ancient World* (New York: The Metropolitan Museum of Art): 168-81.

Bibliography

Roth, H. (1986), *Kunst und Handwerk im frühen Mittelalter* (Stuttgart: Konrad Theiss Verlag).

Sacks, O. (2004), 'In the river of consciousness', *New York Review of Books* 51, 1: 41-4.

Sanden, W. van der and Capelle, T. (2002), *Götter, Götzen, Holzmenschen* (Oldenburg: Isensee Verlag).

Schama, S. (1995), *Landscape and Memory* (New York: A.A. Knopf).

Schröter, P. (1988), 'Zu beabsichtigten künstlichen Kopfumformung im völkerwanderungszeitlichen Mitteleuropa', in H. Dannheimer and H. Dopsch (eds), *Die Bajuwaren von Severin bis Tassilo 488-788* (Munich: Freistaat Baiern): 258-65.

Searle, J.R. (2006), 'Minding the brain', *New York Review of Books* 53, 17: 51-5.

Simons, D.J. and Chabris, C.F. (1999), 'Gorillas in our midst: sustained inattentional blindness for dynamic events', *Perception* 28: 1059-74.

Smith, J.C. (2004), 'Mass communication: prints and printmaking', in *The Northern Renaissance* (London: Phaidon Press): 239-72.

Stafford, B.M. (2007), *Echo Objects: The Cognitive Work of Images* (London: University of Chicago Press).

Stoklund, M. (2003), 'The first runes – the literary language of the Germans', in Jørgensen et al. (eds): 172-9.

Teschler-Nicola, M. and Mitteröcker, P. (2007), 'Von künstlicher Kopfformung', in Anke and Externbrink (eds): 270-9.

Thomas, J. (2006), 'Phenomenologies of landscape and monumentality', in C. Tilley et al. (eds), *Handbook of Material Culture* (London: Sage Publications): 54-7.

Tilley, C. (2004), *The Materiality of Stone* (Oxford: Berg).

Tilley, C., Keane, W., Küchler, S., Rowlands, M. and Spyer, P. (eds) (2006), *Handbook of Material Culture* (London: Sage Publications).

Torbrügge, W. (1971), 'Vor- und frühgeschichtliche Flussfunde: Zur Ordnung und Bestimmung einer Denkmälergruppe', *Bericht der Römisch-Germanischen Kommission* 51-2: 1-146.

Underwood, G. (2005), 'Eye fixations on pictures of natural scenes: getting the gist and identifying the components', in Underwood (ed.): 163-87.

Underwood, G. (ed.) (2005), *Cognitive Processes in Eye Guidance* (Oxford: Oxford University Press).

Vall, R. van de (2003), 'Touching the face: the ethics of visuality between Levinas and a Rembrandt self-portrait', in Farago and Zwijnenberg (eds): 93-111.

Bibliography

Webster, L. (2003), 'Encrypted visions: style and sense in the Anglo-Saxon minor arts, AD 400-900', in C. Karkov and G.H. Brown (eds), *Anglo-Saxon Styles* (Albany, NY: State University of New York Press): 11-30.

Wells, P.S. (1980), *Culture Contact and Culture Change: Early Iron Age Central Europe and the Mediterranean World* (Cambridge: Cambridge University Press).

Wells, P.S. (2007), 'Structures of craft production, society, and political control: late prehistoric and Early Roman temperate Europe', in I. Shimada (ed.), *Craft Production in Complex Societies: Multicraft and Producer Perspectives* (Salt Lake City, UT: University of Utah Press): 137-51.

Wexler, B.E. (2006), *Brain and Culture: Neurobiology, Ideology, and Social Change* (London: MIT Press).

Williams, H. (2006), *Death and Memory in Early Medieval Britain* (Cambridge: Cambridge University Press).

Wilson, S. (2000), *The Magical Universe: Everyday Ritual and Magic in Pre-Modern Europe* (London: Hambledon and London).

Wilson, T.D. (2002), *Strangers to Ourselves: Discovering the Adaptive Unconscious* (Cambridge, MA: Harvard University Press).

Worm, O. (1643), *Danicorum Monumentorum Libri Sex* (Copenhagen: J. Moltkenium).

Yang, X. (ed.) (1999), *The Golden Age of Chinese Archaeology: Celebrated Discoveries from the People's Republic of China* (Washington, DC: National Gallery of Art).

Zanier, W. (1999), *Der spätlatène- und römerzeitliche Brandopferplatz im Forggensee (Gde. Schwangau)* (Munich: C.H. Beck).

Zeki, S. (1998), 'Art and the brain', *Daedalus* 127, 2: 71-103.

Zeki, S. (1999), *Inner Vision: An Exploration of Art and the Brain* (Oxford: Oxford University Press).

Zhuber-Okrog, K. (2007), 'Körperkette mit 52 amulettähnlichen Anhängern', in Anke and Externbrink (eds): 236.

Zürn, H. (1957), 'Zur Chronologie der Alb-Salem-Keramik', *Germania* 35: 224-9.

Zürn, H. (1970), *Hallstattforschungen in Nordwürttemberg* (Stuttgart: Müller & Gräff).

Zwijnenberg, R. and Farago, C. (2003), 'Art history after aesthetics: a provocative introduction', in Farago and Zwijnenberg (eds): vii-xvi.

Index

The words belt buckles, belt hooks, brain, colour, decoration, fibula, image, vessels, visuality and weapons are used throughout the book and are not indexed.

Index

Index

Lightning Source UK Ltd.
Milton Keynes UK
UKOW06f1930040316

269638UK00006B/291/P